Literacy Is Power

How To Change The World Kit

By
Cassandra Lewis Slattery

Cover Art by Peter Slattery

Printed in the United States of America

First Printing, 2012

ISBN 978-0-9886733-1-1

Bastille Arts, LLC

www.BastilleArts.com

For all of the learners I have known.

"Education is the most powerful weapon
we can use to change the world."
–Nelson Mandela

Table of Contents

A Cinderella Story

Cinderella (whose real name is similar, but has been changed in this writing to protect his privacy) is a homeless man from the New York City area. He told me that his mother had actually named him something like Cinderequan, but she never learned how to read or write and didn't notice the mistake on his birth certificate until years later when it was pointed out to her by a school official.

She didn't know how to get the name corrected, so his peers and teachers continued to refer to him by his legal name. His uncle, who was also illiterate, advised him to embrace the name he was given and redefine its meaning. Cinderella did this by beating up anyone who made fun of him.

His resentment towards his family and peers coupled with growing up malnourished, eating only when he got to the food stash before his siblings or when there was enough ramen and peanut butter on stale bread to go around, made learning in school difficult. He couldn't concentrate because he was hungry. He was filled with the kind of hunger that has been lurking for so long it no longer aches, but has turned into a lethargic hollowness that invites depression and dizzy spells, and is often mistaken for apathy.

Cinderella worked hard to redefine his name and fought so many peers that he got a reputation in his neighborhood for being tough and was soon initiated into a gang and dropped out of school. He never learned to read beyond recognizing a few sight words like "milk" and "subway" and the only career opportunities that he was exposed to involved drugs and violence. He made some unfortunate decisions in order to continue participating in the gang lifestyle and instead of earning a high school diploma and a college degree he accumulated a long rap sheet of felony and misdemeanor convictions.

Inside prison, he tried to turn his life around, stopped using drugs and associated with a religious group, but when he was released no legitimate employer would hire him because of his criminal record and his inability to read. The life of poverty that he was born into and the circumstances of his youth still prevent him from securing employment. He is middle-aged and homeless, and owns nothing but his desire to change.

Tragically, Cinderella's story is not unique. There are 775 million people in the world who are illiterate. In America, nearly 50 million people are living in poverty, and according to the most recent National Adult Literacy Survey, 40-44 million American adults can't read. These individuals cannot fill out a job application or read safety instructions or teach their children how to read. Forget the altruistic reasons about why this grim reality should matter, it also costs taxpayers billions of dollars.

The next time a politician of any party complains about the deficit, ask why we haven't tried to teach people how to read. When politicians open their mouths about anything, ask them what they plan to do about the rising number of prison cells, emergency room visits, on-the-job injuries, or unemployment that could be easily addressed by making literacy a priority. Remind them that Cinderella and many others don't vote now, but they may start exercising this right soon because you're out there actually trying to make a difference and you're tired of waiting for more unrealistic policies to pass that only pretend to deal with the problem and are merely window dressing for the next election.

This book is for anyone who wants to change the world. It offers a step-by-step game plan of how to conduct literacy triage so you can start right away and help others empower themselves through literacy.

Chapter 1
Introduction

"Education is all a matter of building bridges." –Ralph Ellison

Have you ever wanted to make a difference, but haven't known how or where to begin? If you can read this book then you can become a literacy leader.

Nearly a quarter of the US population is unable to read, write, or do simple arithmetic on a basic level, according to the report by the US Department of Education's National Center for Education Statistics, *Adult Literacy in America*. These adults have difficulty reading maps, newspaper articles, filling out job applications, balancing a checkbook, understanding safety instructions, or medical dosage information.

People, by nature, are survivors and can adapt to almost any condition. They find ways to survive despite these hurdles and are clever about hiding their disabilities. But often this means confining everyday patterns to what is familiar, living in very small worlds, counting the number of subway stops rather than reading the signs. They avoid visiting new places and rely on what they are told rather than what they read and assess on their own. Are these survivors really living up to full potential as parents or contributing members of society? If they gained literacy skills wouldn't this not only benefit the individual, but also society as a whole?

The United States ranked fifth in the world for adult literacy skills, compared to five other industrialized nations that participated in the Adult Literacy and Lifeskills Survey (ALL). We need to do more than watch fast food chains sidestep this problem by changing words on their cash registers to cartoon images of the product. People should be able to understand what it means to take out a loan, that credit cards are not free money, or why having a bank account is better than using check-cashing stands or saving money under your mattress. And people WANT to learn how to think critically about these things and the news they see on television and why they should encourage their children to stay in school and learn to read when they never did.

Helping people learn how to read can also save taxpayers money. According to ProLiteracy, problems relating to lack of literacy skills cost the US billions of dollars each year, including an estimated $230 billion in healthcare costs and more than $225 billion in lost productivity in the workforce and lost tax revenue due to unemployment.

There is a higher illiteracy rate for those living in poverty, and the problem is perpetuated as children who live in poverty are passed through low-income public schools, not learning how to read and are shut out of higher education and career opportunities that could lift them out of poverty. Many advocacy groups have suggested, and I wholeheartedly agree, that we can begin to attack poverty by building literacy skills for adults and children.

Learning is a lifelong process for all of us, or it should be if we want to keep life interesting. The more we learn the more informed we become, which enables us to make better decisions. The more we know the more confident we become. Gradually, we gain more influence on our own lives and in our communities. Literacy is part of this learning. It's about the ability to decode information and apply it to life in a way that provides the best possible opportunities. Shouldn't this be a tool that everyone has access to?

Promoting literacy is not as simple as passing a few policies about tests or tenure. Of course, the public education system needs serious help, but the problem is more complex and must be addressed on many levels. In fact, almost half of the US adult population struggling with literacy has managed to graduate from high school. We need to fill in the gaps and reach those who have been left out of the system. To read more about how to change the education system, I recommend reading Nikhil Goyal's *One Size Does Not Fit All: A Student's Assessment of School* and Jonathan Kozol's books.

We are living in the Information Age. The Internet connects us with real-time information and more ways to communicate. Distance is no longer the barrier it used to be. This opens up new ways of learning and of teaching.

Just as we are all learners, we are all teachers. Have you ever been frustrated by the injustices of poverty, the criminal justice system, the education system, political corruption, environmental destruction? Have you ever wanted to do something that addresses these problems, but don't have the money to contribute to campaigns or advocacy organizations? This book is about how you can help others to make informed decisions by improving their literacy skills.

The power of the people has even more power if more people are included: more voters, more consumers, and more community leaders. Together, we can make a difference in the world, one hour at a time, one learner at a time. Whether you are already a teacher hoping to improve your skills or whether you've never taught before, this book provides the steps and materials you need to become a literacy leader.

This book won't drown you in statistics or academic jargon. Time is limited and we have much work to do. This book gives concise instructions on structure, assessment, learner-centered curriculum planning, Seven Steps of the Successful Session, and a Literacy Kit. In short, you will learn how to conduct literacy triage.

Literacy triage is the opposite of the cookie-cutter approach, which clearly does not work. Learners are individuals who make decisions in life and should make decisions in the trajectory of their learning.

I have had the honor of witnessing these ideas in action with teen and adult learners who have pulled themselves up by making the decision to improve their literacy skills and their lives.

I created and launched a literacy program at an organization that serves homeless adults in New York City. The program was the only one of its kind, in which all clients who read beneath a 6th grade reading level are provided with free one-on-one literacy instruction. During my tenure as Director of Education the program yielded a 100% success rate. All of my clients who started on a first grade reading level or higher and completed six sessions improved by an average of 1.5 grade levels. Clients who started on a pre-alphabet level required more than six sessions to demonstrate numeric improvement.

This book identifies the best practices for reaching even the most reluctant learners. These ideas can be applied to any population, though I have learned most from working with troubled teens, prison inmates, and homeless individuals.

Secret to success: the best literacy leaders approach the learner as a fellow human being, an equal, and find ways to bridge what the learner already knows with what he will learn.

Chapter 2
What is Literacy?

*"America can no longer take active and engaged literacy for granted. As more Americans lose this capability, our nation becomes less informed, active, and independent minded. These are not qualities that a free, innovative, or productive society can afford to lose." –**Dana Gioia, former Chairman of the National Endowment for the Arts***

Literacy refers to the ability to decode and apply written information to real life. This includes the ability to read and write, and it also includes being able to communicate effectively. It refers to letters and words as well as numbers. Literacy skills include the ability to derive meaning from information and the ability to make informed decisions. It is a tool that we never stop sharpening.

The literacy tool helps us:

o   Read a map so we can get to the job interview
o   Complete the job application without embarrassing mistakes
o   Understand our child's immunization records
o   Comprehend medical dosage directions
o   Negotiate an hourly wage that we can afford to live on
o   Create a budget so paying rent is our first priority each month
o   Balance a checkbook
o   Tell the time and calculate what time we need to leave home in order to get to work on time
o   Use a calendar

- o Identify and understand safety words, such as "caution" and "flammable"
- o Comprehend job ads and distinguish between legit leads and scams
- o Navigate the Internet to look up helpful information, such as job leads
- o Communicate effectively using email and phone
- o Register to vote

Digital Literacy

Digital literacy refers to information technology, including computers. Even the most menial jobs now require some computer skills. Most job leads are found on the Internet, and communication now includes texting, sending emails, and social networking. Many learners did not have the luxury of owning a computer and were left behind when computer skills became the norm. Such learners may not want to pursue a career as an administrative assistant or learn how to type 60 words per minute, but they will want to understand how to navigate the Internet and communicate with email. Once they master these skills, they should work on building comprehension and analytical judgment to discern truth from scam. (See the "Spot the Scam" activity and "Computer Literacy Checklist" in Chapter 11).

For learners who have never used a computer before, get them interested in the Internet by helping them look up something they're passionate about. Google Images is a great way to do Internet research in the form of pictures. Removing the newness and stress of reading makes the Internet accessible and fun.

One of my former clients, a man in his sixties from the Bronx, came to me in tears because he had never used a computer and was terrified that life had passed him by. He feared it was too late to learn this skill. I told him that he was not the first to feel this way, which was true, many clients shared the same fears, and I started by telling him that the Internet was like going on an adventure to another world and I guaranteed he would have fun.

"The Internet browser is your guide in this foreign land of the Internet. This particular browser you're going to click on with the mouse is named Firefox," is how I often start clients with the Internet. I went on to explain that every page on the Internet has a specific address, just like different buildings along the street outside. I asked him to then type "youtube.com" into the address bar and then hit the "return" key. He had already revealed in earlier conversations that he was a classic movie buff. So I told him to type into the search box his favorite movie and see what happened. From that point on he was hooked. He couldn't believe he could see the best moments of his favorite movies for free. By starting with something that was fun and interesting to the learner, he was more receptive to learning other skills later, like email and perusing job ads.

Financial Literacy

Financial literacy is important to master in this time of rampant corruption. Learners need to arm themselves with financial knowledge to protect themselves against mortgage fraud and pernicious credit card interest rates. Financial literacy means understanding how to read a paystub, why check-cashing establishments cost more money than using a checking account, and how to live on a budget. Critical thinking skills are not to be taken for granted. This knowledge is not inherent. It is learned and if the learner missed out on learning this he is vulnerable to scammers.

I have worked with former drug dealers who were considered businessmen in their communities, negotiators of huge sums of cash, before they were locked up. These same dealers, who are much wiser than most in regards to street smarts, were losing 20% of each new legitimate paycheck because they were using a cash-checking place instead of a bank or credit union. It was helpful when we added up how much money had been lost in four weeks to the check-cashing place and then ask them to brainstorm all the things they could have bought with that amount or how much money they could have saved if they had cashed their checks at a credit union or bank.

There is a fear of the unknown BECAUSE it is unknown and the best way to introduce this unknown world is to use the learner's real life issue and directly apply the knowledge to it. This is the core strategy of conducting literacy triage.

Individuals living in poverty don't want to be financially dependent. They want to break out of the cycle of government-subsidized financial confinement. They are tired of the humiliation of having to use food stamps to survive. They want to find ONE full-time job (not two or more) that pays a wage that they can live on and still feed their families. But how do they find those jobs when they can't read and don't even have a GED? How many hours will you have to work when you make $7.25 to save enough to move out of the homeless shelter? And how much will it cost for someone to take care of your kids while you're working one or two full-time jobs? Will this person also take the time to teach your kids how to read, a skill you never learned? These are the real life financial literacy or numeracy questions people are faced with and, even if you do know your multiplication tables, these are difficult questions to answer.

Health Literacy

Health literacy is essential to survival. People need to know how to communicate effectively with their healthcare providers, prepare questions to ask when meeting with a physician, know where to find emergency care, how to dial 9-1-1, how to read medical dosage directions, and how to read their child's immunization records.

Nutrition and eating well and being able to identify food allergies are other important components of health literacy. Often low-income individuals who do not have the luxury of annual check-ups at the doctor's office have undiagnosed illnesses and many end up masking their medical problems with drug addictions. For instance, a former client of mine revealed that his chest pain and the inability to afford medical care led him to take heroin. His heroin addiction masked the pain for years until he was finally admitted to the hospital and his heart problem was diagnosed. He is now in recovery and has been clean and sober for over a year and visits a physician regularly.

Another former client was an elderly man recently diagnosed with diabetes. His doctor gave him a blood sugar kit, but my client didn't understand how to use it and was unable to read the directions. One of our sessions involved reading the instructions together and learning why monitoring blood sugar levels is key to staying alive. We also explored the issue by regularly identifying healthy, low-sodium and low-sugar foods and learned how to cook meals that are aligned with managing diabetes.

How Is It Possible?

How is it possible that so many people in this country and in the world could slip by without learning such fundamental skills? It's a good question and there isn't just one answer.

Super Bowl Champion Dexter Manley shocked the world when he admitted before a Senate subcommittee that he was illiterate. His courage in speaking out inspired many to reevaluate their goals and lent strength to many to admit it was time to make a change. It also highlighted the problem with college sports and how athletes are pushed through the system without ever truly receiving an education.

One of my clients, not as famous as Dexter Manley, but nationally recognized at the peak of his career as a college football athlete, was 33 when he aged out of sports and turned to heroin. He ended up living on the streets for more than a decade and was reading on the first grade reading level when I started meeting with him.

Jimmy Santiago Baca, now a world-renowned poet, novelist, and playwright learned how to read while he was incarcerated. He is a literary hero and a literacy hero. His work is brilliant and a testament to what is possible when an individual makes the courageous decision to change his life and make his dreams a reality. I always include his story and some of his literature in my literacy classes and individual sessions. He is an example of hope and what is possible when one wins the battle against illiteracy.

For some, illiteracy has become the norm for generations and they have adapted and learned how to hide it from the world. One such literacy client was trying to sound out the word "picture." He knew the sounds of each letter, but did not recognize the word because he had always pronounced the word as "pitcher." He explained to me that no one had ever said "piCture." In his case, he was persevering as an adult learner despite at least two generations of illiteracy. His parents and his grandparents couldn't read and this had also altered their pronunciation of words. This may sound bleak, but making observations like this actually helps us address the learning issues of each client. No hurdle is impossible to take on – we just have to know it's there. (See Chapter 9 for more information on phonemic awareness).

Reading and writing are first introduced when the learner is a child and if it isn't presented as fun and as a necessary skill the child will most likely not take to it. If the child doesn't have consistent exposure or a safe environment in which to practice these skills then she may be reluctant to learn. Most public school classrooms are overcrowded and by the time the child gets to the classroom the teacher may not have the time or resources needed to address the problem. Teenagers often have competing interests and chastise each other for wanting to learn and this is another deterrent that inhibits learning.

Sometimes the learner has an undiagnosed learning disability. At the time, and partly because of the shame felt by the learner, it may seem easier to just sneak by without addressing the problem.

Language barriers often create additional hurdles and there are two schools of thought about approaching literacy combined with ESOL (English for Speakers of Other Languages). Some educators believe ESOL learners should first master reading and writing in their native languages before learning these skills in English, while others (myself included) believe it should be up to the learner, based on her specific goals and needs.

In my experience, I've found it to be the best approach to consider each learner as an individual. Each learner arrives with his unique history and experience and reasons for wanting to learn how to read and write at the present time. This is why I believe it's most important for the literacy sessions to be learner-centered and driven by the learner's goals.

Always begin with what you have - with what the learner already knows and build from there, moving towards the individual's specific goals. This will help keep the learner motivated and focused and it is the foundation to conducting literacy triage.

Chapter 3
Where Do I Begin?

*"The function of education is to teach one to think intensively and to think critically... Intelligence plus character - that is the goal of true education." –**Dr. Martin Luther King, Jr.***

Anyone can be a literacy activist. You don't have to necessarily be a teacher by profession. We are all learners and teachers. There is such an overwhelming need for literacy instruction that wherever you are you will find people in need of help. Much of the media focus on literacy is centered on children, which is, of course, very important. However, it should also be just as urgent to reach their parents and families – the adults who were left behind, not to mention the teens dropping out of school. I believe that everyone should have the right to learn and I believe that the individuals who are in the most need of help, those living in the direst circumstances should be helped first.

I fell into this line of work by accident. I was working in the maximum-security mental health unit of a state prison when I first encountered the problem of illiteracy.

It was supposed to be a college internship to learn more about the criminal justice system and "forensic psychology" and ended up being the greatest opportunity of my life. One of the groups of inmates that I co-facilitated was focused on recovery from chemical dependency. The men had been convicted of violent felonies and were grappling with sobriety. It was gradually revealed that most of them could not read past an elementary school level. One of the ways we addressed both their counseling and literacy needs was to read the newspaper and compose poetry and stories together. It was a positive and confidence-building way of using their anger, which can actually be a gift.

They came from troubled homes, sure, everyone's heard that line, but the line no one really gets to is the real issue: in those troubled homes, no one is learning how to read. Public schools in poor neighborhoods do not have the resources to help children catch up the way most teachers would like to. Instead, the children are passed through until their frustration builds to the point where they find it easier to drop out and try to make fast money without ever learning until it's too late that "you end up paying for it anyway – either with money or jail time," to quote one of my former clients.

A lifetime after working in the prison, I worked for an alternative school for troubled teens (also referred to as "at-risk") that had been kicked out of various public junior high and high schools. It was another case in which I was hired to do one thing (answer the phones and manage the attendance) and ended up teaching literacy skills. Every moment there was a teachable one. Even when I was supervising lunch, I found myself correcting the graffiti scrawled across the wall, "This skool sucks." At least two of the three words were spelled correctly. I'd like to say that over time the grammar and poetic resonance of school graffiti improved with my help, but that would be a lie.

The truth is: I learned more from them than they did from me. I learned that more than anything we need to listen to the learners. They don't want to be told what to do or what to memorize for a test, especially when the information seems completely unrelated to their lives. All tests are flawed and the cookie-cutter approach to teaching and learning simply does not work. People are individuals and each one learns differently. They want to learn information that is relevant to their lives and they want to make their own decisions. I learned that aside from directly tutoring a student on how to read, literacy was more easily addressed when it came up in life situations that were applicable to life, like how to write a resume or cover letter. I worked with students on literacy by identifying goals that were positive and relevant.

They taught me that in order to show someone how to empower himself, he must first WANT to. It has to come from the learner, but our expectations and communicating that we expect more from him is the starting point. "You're better than that," is something I would say on a daily basis to various students who acted out. Sometimes having a little validation from a mentor is enough to spark the internal motivation of the learner. When he begins to see that if someone else thinks it's possible, then maybe it really is.

More recently, I created and launched a literacy and basic education program at an organization that helps New York City's homeless population develop job readiness skills. We discovered that it wasn't enough to send clients on interviews because they were unable to get off at the right subway stop and were unable to fill out a job application. So I brought what I had learned from my other experiences and implemented a literacy assessment system that was administered to all participants and those reading under a sixth grade reading level were provided with one-on-one literacy instruction. During my tenure as Director of Education, all of the clients showed improvement and 100% of the clients whose initial placement score was on the first grade reading level or higher improved by at least one reading level within six sessions. Clients who started beneath a first grade reading level required additional literacy sessions.

The clients had literacy goals that included wanting to read to their children or grandchildren, how to fill out a job application, and register to vote.

You don't have to be a full-time teacher to be a literacy leader. There is such an overwhelming need that volunteering just one hour a week would be a meaningful contribution to someone's life.

There are a number of national and local literacy-promoting organizations that pair teachers with learners. The advantage of being referred to a learner through an organization is that the learner has chosen to be there and actually wants help. It's much easier to work with someone who already wants to learn, though everyone has the potential to learn and to teach. (See Chapter 13 for a list of resources).

Another way to reach out to your community is to visit your local library or community center. Libraries are an indispensable resource and are one of the first places those with reading difficulties visit for help. Talk to the staff and find out about their literacy programs or if one isn't yet established, start your own.

Drug treatment programs and homeless shelters are filled with clients who are suddenly sober and in need of something to keep their minds occupied to prevent relapse. Introducing a positive skill that provides a healthy avenue of escape, as reading is, would be invaluable. (See Chapter 11 for a list of contemporary literature and activities that are socially relevant). Any organization dealing with poverty encounters day-to-day issues where literacy instruction would certainly benefit their clients.

Chapter 4
Building Bridges

"Reading a book is like re-writing it for yourself. You bring to a novel, anything you read, all your experience of the world. You bring your history and you read it in your own terms." –Angela Carter

Rapport is the most important ingredient in establishing a constructive teaching relationship. It is not something a person can fake. To build rapport, the literacy leader should come from a place of compassion, with the objective of finding out what the learner already knows in order to work towards what he doesn't know yet.

Everyone has skills and brings something to the table. Even if a person can't read, he knows many other things. As literacy instructors, we connect what is known with what is unknown.

Learning is connecting old associations with new associations. As a literacy leader, you will start with what the learner already knows and build from there. Review is important for building confidence and rapport. This helps the learner relax and become more receptive to new information. Review keeps the learning process fun and engaging. It is also a fundamental part of connecting what the learner knows with what the learner doesn't know.

Don't take anything for granted. Often we assume people already know something when they really don't. Thinking out loud and explaining every little step helps us avoid skipping ahead and creating confusing gaps. Trust that the learner will tell you if she already knows a certain part.

If the learner you are working with has the ability to hear then already you are starting with a skill and you can frame the lessons as review sessions. "You already have the tools because you can hear sounds." And "you already know this because you speak it. Now we're just going to play with sounds in a different way."

It doesn't matter what traits, strengths, or disabilities the learner brings to the table. When we address each learner as an individual we start our process by identifying the abilities the learner has to begin with and we build from those. Those skills serve as the foundation of our process.

I approach my literacy relationships as an exchange of skills. One literacy client had grown up in the south and had a passion for cooking my favorite kinds of foods and has a long-term goal of managing his own restaurant someday. This insight about his interests and goals helped me plan sessions that were centered on cooking. Another teacher, Robyn Olds, who ended up working with him took it even further and created menus, wrote recipes and safety signs for the kitchen, while building his literacy skills.

In the beginning of our literacy relationship I expressed my admiration for his cooking skills and admitted that I knew next to nothing about cooking and was interested in learning. Reinforcing his strength helped him feel more confident and he became less reluctant to learn because the sessions were now framed as an exchange of information.

Other clients have taught me about child rearing, how to put up dry wall, how to fix a clock, how to purchase a lottery ticket, how to speak better in Spanish, and how to download free music on my phone.

Focus on the positive. Always begin with a skill that the learner already has that enables us to frame what we're doing as a "review." This helps us break down the psychological barrier and build confidence and trust.

Chapter 5
Literacy Triage

"I think reading is important in any form. I think a person who's trying to learn to like reading should start off reading about a topic they are interested in, or a person they are interested in." –**Ice Cube**

There isn't enough time to go back to the very beginning and it's patronizing to make a teenager or an adult read about a cartoon dog running after a ball. Learners are struggling to overcome the shame of living with illiteracy and have real problems that need to be addressed immediately, such as understanding medical dosage instructions, navigating the criminal justice system, or finding a job so they can move out of a shelter.

Conducting literacy triage is about drawing literacy instruction from the tasks that are necessary and immediately relevant to the learner's survival, not the other way around. This is where many educational programs go wrong. The cookie-cutter approach does not work and that approach has probably contributed to the reason why the learner dropped out of school.

Everyone has unique patterns of learning. Learners stay engaged in lessons when the lesson directly relates to their immediate interests and needs. The direction and specific material of the sessions comes from the unique individual who is the learner. For instance, I always have materials prepared ahead of time, but I begin each literacy session by asking the learner how he's doing or what's going on right now. Often the learner will be troubled by something or bring up a topic that is already on his mind. Instead of telling him to put it aside, I use his topic or issue as a springboard for learning. It's important for you to be prepared, but also be ready to improvise.

Often you have to sell WHY they should learn, especially when it comes to working with teenagers and others who are already overwhelmed with problems relating to survival. Sometimes we have to connect the dots and remind these learners of specific day-to-day examples of why literacy can help them overcome their problems.

"I just want to find a job. I don't have time to learn how to read." This sentiment comes up often, especially before a client has had her first literacy session. This is not the time to talk about reading for pleasure. It's a teachable moment when you can clarify how reading and writing directly impact the client's goals and ability to survive. In order to get the job, the client must know how to complete a job application and understand what is written on her cover letter and resume. This is also an opportunity to practice appropriate answers to common interview questions. In short, there must be a sense of urgency and a real life application for each literacy lesson.

Remember Abraham Maslow's theory "Hierarchy of Needs" from Psychology 101? The concept puts in order the basic human needs in order of relevance to survival, starting with the Physiological: food, water, breathing, etc., and then moving to the next level, Safety: securing shelter, employment, health, family, etc. The key to incorporating the Hierarchy of Needs into our literacy sales pitch is to associate literacy skills to the Safety level.

Reading, writing, and computing well supports everything that goes into eating, finding shelter, maintaining health, securing housing and employment. Our job is to show each learner the specific ways literacy skills relate to these goals. We do this by sharing specific examples of how literacy instruction has helped other learners.

By mentioning other learners in our sales pitch (not by name, of course) it reinforces the idea that this reluctant learner is not alone. There are other people who are also working to improve their literacy skills, other people who have similar goals. We give examples that show how the ability to read and write well builds confidence and is a necessary tool whether the learner is looking for the name of the subway stop, completing a job application, reading safety instructions at the new job, or negotiating a raise from the boss.

Often the learner will express regret over not having learned these skills before. This presents another teachable moment with the sentiment, "The past has passed. We live in the now and are planning for the future and what is possible." Remind the learner of other things she has learned. For instance, maybe she didn't have an email account or know how to navigate the Internet a few days ago and now she does. Another good point to make is that time passes no matter what and we might as well do something productive while it passes.

In short, our continuous sales pitch must offer specific examples of how building the learner's literacy skills will put the learner on the fast track to reaching his goals. Literacy triage builds lessons from real life issues that the learner is presently experiencing, grounding the learning process in practical application.

Chapter 6
Keep It Real / The First Session

"If you don't become an actor you'll never be a factor." – **Lupe Fiasco**

It is important to keep the learning process centered on the specific short and long term goals of the learner. This keeps the sessions relevant to life and arms the learner with the skills she needs to overcome barriers right away. Keeping sessions goal-centered also reinforces the consistency of the sessions. It is less likely the learner will miss weekly sessions when she can directly apply the skills to life.

Sessions should be held in a quiet and safe environment, such as a living room, a meeting room inside a library, a classroom, or in an office after hours when there will be no interruptions. It should be held in privacy. The learner does not want anyone else to overhear his difficulty with reading.

It's best to hold sessions once or twice a week and each should be one to two hours long. Most people I have worked with have short attention spans and difficulty committing to anything longer than an hour, so I book them for one-hour time slots but when I can I try to allow for the session to go longer. In other words, I trick them into meeting longer than an hour, but never force them to meet longer than an hour. I allow flexibility with my time so that if the learner wants to meet longer than an hour she can. Whatever your schedule preferences, it's best to meet at the same time each week and encourage consistency. Get the learner into the habit of meeting. This consistency contributes to her improvement and she will progress much faster.

Preparing For Your First Literacy Session

The first session will be devoted to building rapport. It is not wasted time to get to know the learner and find out about his life. This information will help you create a learner-centered curriculum.

Here are some questions and conversational prompts to get you started:

1) *What was your experience with education like when you were younger?*

Was the learner frustrated? Did he drop out? What in particular was frustrating for him? Often a client will reveal a learning disability at this point, if it has ever been diagnosed.

2) *It's never too late to earn your GED. In fact, adult learners who earn their GEDs increase their annual salary by thousands of dollars. Sometimes there's some catching up to do before we can get that valuable piece of paper, so what are some areas that you'd like to work on first?*

This will help you start to identify problem areas and also areas that interest the learner, indispensable information as you prepare for each session.

3) *What do you do for a living? Or, what would you like to do for a living?*

Understanding what the learner's day-to-day life is like will help you identify goals and areas to work on. For instance, if the learner is a janitor you may want to address whether he knows key safety words (See Chapter 11 for the Safety Words List) and knows not to mix things like ammonia and bleach. Expand his bank of sight words to include "caution" and "poisonous."

4) *What is your dream job? Or, if money weren't an issue, what would you spend your days doing?*

This information will help you learn more about the learner's interests and identify long-term goals.

5) *Are there any upcoming issues you'd like to work on?*

Often clients need help filling out forms like, registering to vote or signing a new lease.

6) *How would you describe your long-term goals? Where do you imagine yourself five or ten years down the road?*

Clients often have difficulty imagining long-term goals. Help them imagine what they could be working towards, whether it's being promoted to manager at their job, reading books to their children or grandchildren, finding a job that allows them financial independence, or writing their memoirs. Everyone has dreams. We just have to be reminded of them at times.

7) *Can you name some short-term goals that you would like to work towards?*

These goals will more clearly relate to what will be covered in literacy sessions and may include items from the Literacy Goals Checklist:

_____ Know the letters and sounds of each letter in the alphabet
_____ Write name and address
_____ Read a subway map
_____ Complete a job application
_____ Identify and understand key safety words
_____ Write a resume
_____ Compose a cover letter
_____ Read and comprehend job ads
_____ Create an email account
_____ Navigate the Internet to find job leads
_____ Use a dictionary
_____ Write a check
_____ Understand a paystub
_____ Balance a checkbook
_____ Create a budget
_____ Tell time
_____ Use a calendar
_____ Read and understand a New Employee Manual
_____ Understand prescription directions
_____ Read and understand medical instructions

Start each session by clarifying the learner's expectations and goals. Each session should be grounded in the learner's life and this will keep him coming back and will make reading more interesting for him.

After getting to know the new learner, I begin the literacy relationship by reading the poem, "Hold Fast To Dreams," by Langston Hughes. This poem has an uplifting message, rhymes, and uses simple language, though most learners are unfamiliar with the word "barren" and stumble on "broken-winged." Address the words as they arise in the poem or mention them before the learner reads the poem. Depending on the learner's comfort level, I either read the poem to him or ask him to read it to me.

Then we discuss the meaning of the poem. Langston Hughes' poem is about how holding onto our dreams or goals is what pulls us through the difficult times. No matter how difficult life can be, at least we have our dreams. Our dreams are valuable and no one can take them away from us. This hope is our roadmap, guiding us through life. The poem is a reminder to the client that he is working towards his goals by working on his literacy skills and it begins the literacy relationship with an encouraging tone.

Chapter 7
We Are All Learners

*"The burden of poverty isn't just that you don't always have the things you need, it's the feeling of being embarrassed every day of your life, and you'd do anything to lift that burden." –**Jay-Z***

We are learning about the learner's life, his goals, and beginning to observe his unique problem patterns. But first, consider what the learner does well and how each session can be an exchange of skills.

Shame is one of the biggest barriers the literacy instructor must overcome. People who can't read and write well know they can't, but they haven't yet experienced how learning these skills will actually improve their lives. These people may not be able to read or write well, but they are smart. They have managed to survive without revealing this drawback. What the adult or teen learner may lack in literacy skills she has made up for in interpersonal skills. They are usually exceptionally gifted at reading people, subtle social cues and the underlying psychology of situations.

This is where we will first connect with the learner - on a human-to-human level. We must remember to approach the literacy session as a meeting of two equal individuals who are working towards building something together.

Life is all about change. Events happen every moment. We are constantly taking in new information. As literacy leaders we employ empathy to make literacy skills relevant in the learners' lives. We learn about the learner's interests, and we also learn about the learner's specific problem patterns.

Problem patterns are mistakes we make repeatedly. For instance, I used to always spend a third of my paycheck on payday, even when I knew I shouldn't. Even though I've improved upon this behavior, I could certainly benefit from some financial literacy instruction on how to budget better. When it comes to identifying literacy problem patterns, we have to pay close attention to where the learner is going wrong.

Part of paying attention in this way is allowing the learner some room as she makes mistakes and taking the time to assess as a literacy leader where to begin, what to address first. We do not address everything at once because it would discourage the learner and hinder the learning process.

Our main objective is to observe problem patterns in the learner's reading habits. Does he mix up the sounds of "short a" and "short e" or skip over certain words? What do the words have in common that he is skipping? Are you noticing that the learner cannot sound out words that are longer than one syllable? To best serve the learner, we need to learn where they are experiencing difficulty.

Here are some areas of focus. (See Chapters 9 and 11 for activity material).

o   Can the learner recite the alphabet?
o   Can the learner identify the five vowels: a, e, i, o, u?
o   Does the learner know the short and long sounds of each vowel?
   —   Offer words that demonstrate the sound and ask if the learner can identify whether it's a short or long sound

and of which vowel. For instance, "short a" words could include "cat" and "apple."
- Write the words or construct with word tiles for the learner to visualize after the sound connections have been established.

o Can the learner recognize rhymes?
- Say three words aloud and ask the learner which of the two rhyme and then write them out for the learner.
- Write three words and have the learner read them aloud and identify the two that rhyme. For example, "king, ring, and bat." "King" and "ring" rhyme.
- Encourage the learner to brainstorm other words that rhyme.

o Is the learner dropping just the ends of words, such as "s" at the end of plural words or "ing" in gerund words, like "singing?"
- Point this out and offer examples of words that end in "s" and the same word that doesn't end in "s" so that the learner can see and hear the difference and understand when each is used.
- Often learners who drop endings have difficulty understanding subject and verb agreement and may have trouble with blending sounds. Reinforcing the individual sounds of each letter will help the learner persevere.

o How is the learner's handwriting?
- The learner may write in all capital letters or write certain letters backwards. If this is the case, compliment what she does well in her writing first, and then share your observation that she is mixing and matching lower and upper case letters and then offer a written example of every letter in capital and lower case form. Have the learner practice writing each.

After we start noticing problem areas, we return to the learner's strengths – what she does well and build from there. Building from what she knows, we can then create a learner-centered curriculum.

Chapter 8
Measuring Progress

"Believe in life! Always human beings will live and progress to greater, broader, and fuller life." –W.E.B. Du Bois

One of the first things I learned in Brother Brian Dybowski's Tests & Measurements course in college was that all tests are flawed and most are socioeconomically biased. However, they can help us as educators if we don't put too much stock in them and use them only as a tool, not the only tool, but A tool – one of many –in our assessment of where the learner is initially and to gauge how far he has progressed within a certain period of time.

Most people who are in need of literacy instruction have already been traumatized by the education system and probably hate tests. Therefore, our object as literacy leaders should be to use tests sparingly and only when absolutely needed. They should be primarily used as a tool to continue building the learner's confidence and to help shape literacy sessions so they are tailored to the specific goals and needs of the learner. A placement test can help the literacy leader understand which reading level to work from and prepare level-appropriate materials for each session.

To best serve the learner, you will want to establish a baseline from which to measure progress, but how you decide to do this will depend on what you plan to do with the data.

If you are working with an organization that wants to establish a literacy program, then you should first figure out where your fundraising efforts will be directed (see Chapter 12, Fundraising). If you plan to pursue state or federal funding, then you will most likely have to implement a standardized testing system, such as TABE or CASAS. But if most of your fundraising efforts will be drawn from private foundations, organizations, and individuals, then you have more freedom when it comes to measuring progress.

Measuring progress has been widely written about and sometimes it seems there are too many options to sift through and certainly too much emphasis placed on tests. What I've learned comes from my work experiences and immensely helpful discussions with Todd Evans and David Whitaker at ProLiteracy and Steve Hannum at the Literacy Council of Central Alabama.

There are three basic forms of literacy assessment: 1) standardized, 2) materials-based assessment, and 3) performance assessment. Each method has strengths and weaknesses and all of these methods should be supplemented with a more qualitative demonstration of progress, such as each learner's writing portfolio and a descriptive summary of progress. For instance, "Johnny D. came to us unable to recite the alphabet and now he is able to read to his children."

Standardized tests, the most widely used form of assessment, are good for presenting straightforward reading grade-level numbers, like, "We served 200 people in the past two years and 96% increased their reading levels by one and a half grades." This form of measurement is more uniform, but it does not show the full picture, and if the learner is operating on a pre-alphabet level, she will need more time to show progress on a standardized test. Her progress would be better represented by performance-based or even materials-based assessments in addition to more descriptive support materials, like a writing portfolio. Another drawback of standardized tests is that they take hours to administer and can discourage and further traumatize the learner.

Materials-based assessment can paint a similar picture as standardized tests, but require less time of the learner and are more "user friendly" than standardized tests. Placement tests that correlate to the reading levels within a series of literacy workbooks are an example of materials-based assessment. Be sure to verify that the placement levels roughly correlate to grade reading levels so that you can offer this as a reporting tool. Placement tests are good for determining which level to start from. You'll want to administer the placement test every ten to twelve weeks, or according to your admissions process. Decide on a set period of time that you will administer the placement test in order to keep your data consistent.

Performance-based assessment requires the learner to demonstrate or apply the knowledge they have learned to a series of tasks. You could establish a Real Life Literacy Goal Checklist or the Computer Literacy Checklist, like those presented in Chapter 11, and report based on these goal-based achievements.

Performance-based assessment reporting would include information like, "After fifty hours of instruction, Sam S. can now balance a checkbook, read a subway map, and complete a job application." Or, "Of the fifty clients we served so far, 100% have achieved at least two of the Real Life Literacy Goals."

If you are not starting up your own literacy program or serving a large number of learners, I recommend simply establishing a series of real life goals with the learner, based on his specific needs and interests and building each session around those. To supplement those goals, I would invest in a workbook series and administer the placement test to help you select level-appropriate materials.

All of the methods of assessment should be supported with a writing portfolio of each learner's progress. This is a powerful way to demonstrate progress and tell the funders a story in a way that is visual and more personal. Also, and most importantly, it is valuable to the learner to look back at a writing portfolio and see how far he's come.

All tests are flawed, yet they can provide a baseline idea of where the learner is starting from, mark levels of improvement, and help the literacy leader make sure he is using the appropriate material to suit the learner's needs.

Ideally, progress should be measured in three ways: 1) by specific goals set by the learner, 2) by qualitative improvement (e.g., handwriting and spelling in a journal or writing portfolio), and 3) by quantitative measurement (e.g., reading grade or workbook levels).

Chapter 9
Fun With Phonics & Comprehension

"A little learning, indeed, may be a dangerous thing, but the want of learning is a calamity to any people." –Frederick Douglass

Anyone who can read can be a literacy leader. You don't have to have an advanced degree in linguistics or education. Literacy is about decoding and interpreting information, and in order to do that we must first ensure that the learner is armed with the tools to attack unfamiliar words.

The specific materials you use to address phonics should depend on the learner's interests and goals. For instance, if the learner is applying for a maintenance job, you could use the Safety and Job Application Word Lists from Chapter 11 to strengthen the learner's **phonemic awareness,** the ability to hear and produce individual units of sound.

Returning to the idea of conducting literacy triage, these are the areas that should be assessed first: consonants and vowels.

Part 1: Consonants

Can the learner correctly identify the name of each consonant in the alphabet? Does he know the sound of each letter? Listen for troublesome areas. There is a subtle difference between "t" and "d." How confident is the learner in their pronunciation?

Knowing the sounds of each letter is the first step of being able to decode information. If the learner can hear and produce the sounds of each letter then he will then be able to correctly blend the letters together and dissect unfamiliar words by using these skills to sound out the words.

Communicate with the learner. The learner will most likely tell you if she doesn't know all of the letters.

Here's how I present this assessment to a client:

"I know that you already know this, but I am trying to learn where we should start from. We may have to backtrack and review things you already know. Sometimes when doing this exercise, a learner will teach me that we need to review the sounds of certain letters."

Usually the learner is more receptive when it is presented as a review and an exercise that teaches the teacher. Ask the learner to identify and demonstrate the sound of each consonant. Make a note to yourself of any problem consonants.

Later, when you have established that the learner can differentiate the sounds of each consonant you will address **consonant blends**, two or more consonant letters blended together. Some examples of consonant blends are: *tr, bl, cl, fl, gr* as in *truck, blend, flew, grow,* and so on. **Digraphs**, or a pair of letters that make one unit of sound, like "ch" or "sh" will also need to be explored with the learner.

Often learners who have trouble with blending sounds have difficulty spelling. So if the learner mentions her difficulty spelling, that may be a clue to investigate how well she blends sounds. Before we can work on **blending** the sounds, we make sure the learner understands the individual sounds. Another way to demonstrate how letters and their sounds blend together is by **segmenting**, or breaking a word down into individual sounds and syllables. "Fall" becomes "/f/, /a/, and /l/."

Part 2: Vowels

After you review the consonants, move on to the vowels.

Often problems are rooted in a confusion of vowel sounds. I present this assessment as "backtracking" to the learner. Explain that you're simply trying to solve a mystery with the learner and the clues to finding the culprit can be found by listening to how the learner produces the sound of each letter.

Does the learner know the **short and long sounds** of each vowel?

Sometimes the learner only knows some of the sounds, but will confuse two or more of the vowel sounds, like "short a," and "short e." This discovery is essential to creating positive and productive literacy sessions.

Does the learner understand what you mean when you say short and long? Give examples, "short a" is in the beginning of "apple," and "long a" is in "ape." One way to help the learner remember the difference is to explain that the long sound of the vowel can be found by saying the vowel's name.

During this assessment exercise, I ask the learner to name examples of words with short and long vowels and I write them down so he can see the correct spelling and connect the sound with the visual image. This helps the learner's focus stay on the sound part of the exercise. On your paper, make a list of words under each category: Short A, Long A, Short E, Long E, Short I, Long I, Short O, Long O, Short U, and Long U.

Here is an example:

Short A	Long A
apple, at, mad, glad, sand	ate, plate, mate, rake, ache
Short E	Long E
end, Ed, bed, red, fleck	eat, feet, greet, keep, meet
Short I	Long I
in, imp, kin, win, mitt	I, ice, tide, idle, idol, fly*
Short O	Long O
on, off, dock, clock, lot	open, toe, row, load, road
Short U	Long U
up, under, mutt, ugly, duck	unite, university, unicorn, you, fuse

The word "fly" falls under the "sometimes y" category. If the learner mentions a "y" word like this, just explain that even though "y" is a consonant, it sometimes makes a sound like a vowel.

If vowels are not yet familiar to the learner, begin by working with just the short vowel sounds of each and move onto long vowel sounds in later sessions, after the short ones have been mastered.

Depending on the examples that the learner comes up with you can expand upon concepts like **vowel digraphs** or a combination of vowels that make a single vowel sound, like "oa" in "road" or "ea" in "bread." Don't overwhelm the learner with words like "digraph," just focus on the sounds. Can the learner identify the long and short sounds? Note the areas for improvement. Learners of all levels often need to review vowels. Identifying problem areas of sound can save time later.

Identifying **syllables** or breaking down words into sound units is another way to reinforce the learner's ability to segment and sound out words. Rhyming is another way to explore the sounds and structures of similar words. Words like "dream" and "seem" offer good examples of vowel digraphs that make the same sounds, but have different spellings.

Compound words like "background" and "grandmother" help reinforce how segmenting words into syllables and sounds builds spelling skills.

Words like "hay" or "cow," which have two vowel sounds occurring in the same syllable are known as **gliding vowels** or **diphthongs**, but again there's really no reason to bog down the learner with these terms, unless she expresses an interest in knowing them.

By the end of this activity, even if you decide to only focus on the short vowel sounds, you and the learner will have brainstormed a number of example words. Be sure to praise the learner for coming up with so many words.

Depending on the level of need, you may not have to study each letter and its sound. You will get a sense if the learner "gets" the sound and letter connection. Obviously, if there is a lot of confusion in this area, then that is a good indicator that you will need to start from naming and sounding each individual letter.

If the learner still needs to work on correctly naming and identifying the sound of each letter, I recommend doing a flashcard art project with the learner. Using index cards and cut out images from magazines or printed from the Internet, on each card write the capital and lower case letter on one side and on the other side paste or draw a picture with the written name of a word that begins with the letter. Also, using a sand tray is good for adding a tactile approach. Have the learner draw the letter in the sand while saying, "'A' sounds like /a/, and so on for each letter.

If the learner is more advanced and can already identify and produce sounds for each letter, then move onto activities that reinforce his blending and segmenting skills, spelling, and reading comprehension.

Helpful Phrases

It is important to encourage the learner with positive guidance as she builds the skills to sound out words. Give the learner time to try to sound out words and offer clues instead of simply telling the learner what the word is. Remind them that if the word has a "**silent e**" at the end, the vowel will stretch into a long sound.

"**Close**," is always a good thing to say after a learner tries to read a word and hasn't quite nailed it.

"**Take your time**," is a standby affirmation to the learner that she can take the time to think about it and sound it out. This is not a race, it's a process that will definitely show results, but only if the instructor offers patience.

"**Try saying it in slow motion**," is another way of reminding the client to slow down and really try to hear each sound in the word.

"You know this. You're just over-thinking it." This phrase is another supportive way of praising the learner's ability while also raising what seems to be the central issue to most learning blocks: confidence. Often the biggest hurdle in learning is helping the learner get out of his own way. When we question our ability and tell ourselves that we're always wrong, we won't be able to see the answer, even when it's right in front of us. This principle is why the best teachers are also good counselors, and vice versa.

Comprehension

Reading comprehension refers to the level of understanding of text. Does the learner remember what he just read? What happened in the story? Can the learner infer meaning from the story? Is the learner picturing the characters and actions as they are happening? One of the reasons using socially or personally relevant reading material is important is because this helps the learner better picture in his mind what he's reading as he's reading it.

Comprehension applies to reading stories, manuals, directions, or anything else. Our role as literacy leaders requires us to identify where the learner is having difficulty connecting to the material. In many ways, this is where the real investigation begins.

Learners, who have learning disabilities or struggle with comprehension, should first be praised for what they are doing well. Often learners will be able to read a story perfectly, but won't be able to remember anything they just read or only remember parts of it. Encourage them to look back in the reading to try to find the answers.

Sometimes it is helpful to have the learner read one sentence at a time out loud. Ask the learner what's going on in that sentence. What does the character look like in his mind and does he picture what is happening? Remind the learner that one of the most fun parts of reading is what we bring to what we read. Our imaginations make the words come alive and we should be picturing the action as it unfolds. Sometimes the learner will need some help in activating his imagination and picturing the action of each sentence as he reads it. If this is the case, have him read only one sentence at a time and discuss what he sees as he's reading it, rather than reading the entire passage first. Understand that this process takes time and you may not get through an entire story or passage in one session and that's okay. In fact, it's necessary.

As comprehension is related to phonemic awareness, many learners drop the endings of words, and this throws off the meaning of what is being read. Often this happens when a learner is so focused on identifying the base word that he misses the ending or maybe he hasn't made the connection between tenses of a word and how a word's ending or spelling changes its meaning.

Plural endings involve adding an "s" or "es" or "ies" to a word. Some examples of plural endings are dollars, restaurants, bills, classes, dresses, bills, groceries, and salaries.

Clarifying **verb tenses** is key to building comprehension skills. Words like "am, are, was, heard, known, and written," are examples of common problem verb tense words.

Eventually, much later in the process, when the learner has mastered the other points, you will want to explore the learner's understanding of **contractions** like "isn't, doesn't, you're, and "weren't."

Be sure to address these issues after you have praised the learner for identifying the base word. Start with the positive, something the learner has done well before offering a correction.

Handwriting

We live in the digital age and I recommend incorporating computers into literacy sessions, but also learners should still practice writing words and sentences by hand. Tasks like completing a state identification form or a job application require that the writer print clearly. In the case of a job application, it serves as a first impression of the learner to the prospective employer.

Many learners mix up lower and upper case letters. Sometimes the learner will have to relearn how to print letters. I find it helpful to explore this by offering a writing prompt (see Chapter 11 for examples) and observing whether the learner needs to practice her handwriting.

Don't correct the spelling, grammar, and the handwriting at the same time. When conducting literacy triage, we have to focus on the most immediate problem at a time and help the learner improve her skills with encouragement and constructive instruction. It is not constructive or helpful to overwhelm the learner with all of the problems. Prioritize which task to begin with by referring back to the learner's goals and most immediate task at hand. If the learner is looking for work, then begin with handwriting and practice filling out job applications together.

If handwriting is something the learner needs to work on, write both the capital and lowercase letter for the learner to copy on lined paper. Show him how to write each letter with easy strokes. Have the learner copy a few of each letter and then encourage him to practice writing each letter at home. Eventually, muscle memory will kick in, but it may be slow going in the beginning.

Just as words are composed of letters that represent blended sound units, literacy is an amalgamation of phonemic awareness, comprehension, and application. Identifying sounds and the correct spelling of words are key to strengthening the learner's literacy skills. Keeping the materials interesting and relevant to the learner's life will help you prioritize the activities in your literacy triage kit and what the learner takes from each literacy session will stick and motivate the learner to continue learning.

Chapter 10
Seven Steps For A Successful Session

*"Live as if you were to die tomorrow. Learn as if you were to live forever." –**Mahatma Gandhi***

This chapter presents the core philosophy behind conducting literacy triage and creating a learner-centered curriculum. In each session you will provide opportunities for the learner to make decisions and direct the focus of each lesson on the learner's specific interests and goals. If you incorporate the Seven Steps into each session, I guarantee you will be the catalyst of change that can boost even the most reluctant learners. The Seven Steps make the learning process fun, relevant to real life, and will yield success.

Step One: Meet The Learner On The Level

Always begin with what the learner already knows. To do this, we must first determine the reading level upon which the learner is presently functioning. Can the learner read at all? Does he know the alphabet? Which sight words does he already know? Does he know how to sound out words or is he relying on memory alone? Does he know the short and long vowel sounds of each vowel?

The purpose of approximating the learner's present reading level is to help you, the literacy leader, prepare activities that will not be too easy or too difficult for the learner. Numeric values are only helpful for measuring progress when writing reports for fundraising. Otherwise, numbers can be distracting and discouraging to the learner. Why would someone want to know she is reading on a third grade level? Would the learner's knowledge of that fact help her progress or would it be another assault on her self-esteem?

Depending on which measurement you decide to use (see Chapter 8), I recommend keeping the score to yourself unless the learner really wants to know.

Placement tests should be administered regularly to keep the data consistent. Most learners require about 100 hours of instruction before they will progress to the next reading level. However, by using this learner-centered literacy triage strategy I have seen reading level progression happen much faster – within six sessions. Also, you don't want to wait too long between administering the placement test in case the learner stops attending sessions. While working with formerly homeless and drug-addicted clients I often missed out on obtaining follow-up testing scores due to a client's sudden relapse or disappearance. So I would test more frequently, and with this method of literacy triage teaching, yielded astonishingly high success rates.

Ideally, if you are working with more motivated clients who have consistent attendance, you will see their test scores steadily increase. In this case, you would administer the placement test every ten to twelve weeks.

Learners, particularly learners who are operating beneath a first grade reading level, those who are still learning the sounds of each letter, will take longer to progress. Everyone, 100% of your clients will improve somehow because no one is going to read less or worse than they did before they started investing thought and time in improving their literacy skills.

Another great way of assessing reading skills, particularly of **sight words** (words that the learner has memorized by sight) is to administer Dr. Fry's lists of words, available for free on the Internet. These are a compilation of the most common words found in published material and are widely respected and utilized by teachers. The lists help you assess which words the learner knows and which ones she still needs to learn and provide a starting point to build from.

If you prefer to use a placement test, then you will want to invest in buying a series of workbooks to use as backup to the *Literacy Is Power* activities because the placement score correlates to the workbook levels within the series and helps you mark when it is time for the learner to transition to the next workbook. (See Chapter 8 for more about testing options).

Before I administer the initial placement assessment, I tell my clients, "This isn't really a test. This is just an assessment that helps me know which materials I should bring when we meet. It's really about keeping me in check with what I'm doing."

In summary, Step One is about identifying a baseline snapshot of the learner's current level of functioning from which to measure progress. You will refer to this baseline level as you prepare for each session or if it is time to re-test, then you will administer a new placement test during the session.

Step Two: Goals

In order to make each literacy session interesting and relevant to the learner's life, we will find out about her life and identify short and long-term goals that will be addressed in each session. Is the learner studying for a citizenship test or a driving test? Does he want to improve his map reading skills in order to keep his job as a courier? Does she want to be able to properly administer medicine to her sickly daughter?

Most of the first session will be spent building rapport and at the root of the rapport is discussing what the learner hopes to accomplish in each literacy session. Are there specific areas the learner would like to focus on? For example, many clients I've worked with have had children and grandchildren to whom they wish to read or help with homework.

Short-term goals are more immediate in time frame, like filling out a job application or DMV form and long-term goals take more time to accomplish, like earning a GED, landing a new job, or being able to read for pleasure.

The reasoning behind building each session from the learner's specific goals is to keep the sessions relevant to the learner's life, keeping them interested and helping them apply the information to real life events. Progress becomes more apparent to both the literacy leader and learner.

Step Two is about reviewing and working towards both short and long-term goals. In the first session we find out about the learner's educational background and goals relating to real life issues, including employment, education, and family. Every session addresses short-term goals, praises goal

attainment, and over time the discussion progresses towards reaching long-term goals.

Step Three: Learner-Centered Curriculum

I always promise that if I can get the learner to attend one session, he'll come to all of them. Learners are filled with shame and fear of the unknown and deciding to meet with an instructor is a big step. With any major step in life, the individual is filled with ambivalence. We as literacy leaders can help lift this burden by asking the learner questions about their goals and dreams that help steer them back towards embracing this new change.

The reason why clients keep coming back and find it easier to stick to the commitment they've made to improve their literacy skills while using the strategy presented in this book is because every session is tailored to the specific learner. It's all about them. The lessons come out of real life issues they are confronting. They have no choice but to be interested while they learn how to read and write while taking care of what may otherwise be an impossible challenge.

For example, I often help clients complete DMV applications and have side lessons about spelling or the correct way to write a phone number as we complete the form together. The lessons happen organically and seem casual, and therefore, less frightening when they arise during conversation about the learner's work or family.

I always begin each session by checking in with the learner. How is he doing? What's on his mind today? If he is concerned about something that happened at work, we can use that issue to build that session's lessons from. What did he say to his boss? What should he say next time? This approach addresses both the problematic issue and literacy hurdles.

Don't confuse building rapport and allowing the organic flow of lessons from life issues with the importance of being prepared. Each session should be prepared ahead of time with more material prepared than you will actually need. Improvisation will happen in a successful session, but it's key to have back up material prepared in case the conversation doesn't flow as naturally as it did in previous sessions. Workbooks provide support material, but are optional and secondary to our main objective, which is to identify and address patterns of problem areas in regards to phonics and phonemic awareness (see Chapter 9). Every lesson should be grounded in real life application (i.e. all about them and what they are going through right now).

o Begin with review. Everything should be about connecting what is known with what is unknown. This builds confidence and helps the learner relax and be able to take in new ideas.
o Literacy includes all forms of communication. Lessons should involve reading and writing and also incorporate listening and speaking skills.
o Exercises that are hands-on are helpful (letter tiles, Scrabble, stamp art, sand trays, matching games, teacher dictating a story to the learner who writes it. See Chapter 11 for a list of activities). Teach the same idea in multiple ways until it sticks.
o Improvise. If the client arrives fixated on something that is going on in life, work with it and use that issue to build upon. Connect what they're already thinking about with what they need to learn.

Step Three: Creating A Learner-Centered Curriculum planning is about keeping the focus of every session on the learner's immediate needs and interests by being ready to improvise during the session.

Step Four: Writing Portfolio

The best way to demonstrate the learner's reading and writing improvement is by examining her work on multiple levels. You should track progress quantitatively and qualitatively: with a numeric placement test score, fulfillment of specific goals set by the learner, and with a writing portfolio. Every session should include at least one activity that involves writing and this should be added to the learner's writing portfolio, a collection of the learner's writing over time.

We cannot tackle all of the problems at once in each writing sample. You will see that the learner has difficulty with spelling and grammar. The first letter of the sentence will not be capitalized or every letter will be capitalized. There will be missing words, unidentifiable words, etc. Returning to the concept of conducting literacy triage, we must pick one issue at a time, one word at a time, and often one letter at a time. The writing portfolio is simply a collection of writing to present the learner's improvement over time. There will be errors and this is just a part of the story you are presenting.

The learner should complete a writing exercise during each session (see Chapter 11). After the learner completes the writing exercise, ask him to read it aloud. Sometimes he will notice on his own that words are missing and he may want to go back and write them in. Have the learner read his work out loud so you understand what he intended to write and no matter what is written, begin the feedback session with a compliment. Notice something positive that the learner did well and start the feedback with this constructive observation. Maybe her handwriting was better than it was last time or better than you expected it to be. Maybe there was a lot of feeling behind the story written even if everything was misspelled and multiple words were missing.

A common reaction I have to writing is, "Wow, that was a great story," or "I know it's hard to think of something on the fly, but you did a tremendous job. Most people wouldn't be able to come up with such a well thought out response." This positive reaction should be true – it should be something the learner did well and you are leading with that before you offer suggestions for improvement.

After you lead with a compliment, then you can add that there are still a few spelling issues or handwriting issues, but pick one. Don't overwhelm the learner with all the things he's doing wrong. Find something he is doing right and start with that. Then, on a new page, start a new exercise that offers corrections.

One time a learner wrote a story about reuniting with his son after spending most of his son's life in prison. It was a touching story, but it was written in fragments with many spelling errors. When he finished reading the story to me, I told him how I was moved by his story and excited to add it to his writing portfolio and then on a new page I showed him the spelling of "ours" and "hours" and we came up with sentences that used each correctly. We did this on a new page so he wouldn't develop negative associations with the writing part of each session. He looked back on his portfolio months later and noticed his own mistakes and commented on how much his spelling has improved. The portfolio helps the learner build confidence and illustrates how much he has improved over time. It benefits the learner and the literacy leader alike.

Step Two of having a successful session is the learner's contribution to her writing portfolio. The learner will complete a writing exercise during each session and will perhaps also be keeping a journal during her outside time that can also be used as part of the collection. Each piece of writing should be dated to mark when the improvements happened. The portfolio should be organized in chronological order and include a summary of progress presented with each client's portfolio, to further highlight the progress.

Step Four: During each session, the learner will complete a writing activity for the writing portfolio.

Step Five: Read Outside of Session

Learners show the most progress when they invest outside time in their reading and writing. The more learners think about reading and practice reading, the faster their skills will strengthen.

Encourage the learner to try to read twenty minutes a day, whether it's the newspaper, the latest issue of *The Change Agent*, a romance novel, or a GED-prep textbook and have the learner record it on his weekly Reading Log. The reading material will depend on the learner's reading level. For learners who are still struggling with correctly identifying vowel sounds, I recommend making copies of ghost stories from children's books without directly revealing they are from children's books. Or, print out a one-page "Weird News" story and have that be the week's reading assignment rather than giving a low functioning learner a book that is on an inappropriate reading level. For learners who are on the fourth or higher reading level, find out if there are specific books or topic areas of interest and help the learners obtain a library card and check out the books.

If you want to add an incentive, make a deal with the learner. Tell him he will receive a small prize, like a movie ticket, when he has achieved a certain number of reading hours. Here is a sample reading log that I used with my clients:

WEEKLY READING LOG

Name: _____

Dates: _____

Please list the titles of the books, newspapers, magazines, and other materials you read this week. Also, please list the amount of time you spent each day reading.

Titles	Mon	Tue	Wed	Thu	Fri	Sat	Sun

Favorite facts or stories of this week:

Other notes:

Step Six: Build Spelling and Vocabulary

Each session should include spelling activities, which can include flashcards, Robyn's Fill-It-In Game (Chapter 11), and quizzing the learner on problem words.

Spelling skills are integral to phonemic awareness and as the learner improves his spelling skills, his ability to "sound out" unfamiliar words will improve. These exercises build confidence and are an area where the learner and literacy leader alike can directly witness the learning progress.

Compile a Word Bank or a collection of words that the learner will 1) learn to spell correctly, 2) understand the meaning of and 3) apply in a sentence and connect its relevance to real life. Chapter 11 includes a Job Application Word List and a Safety Word List.

Step Six is all about the spelling! Each session should incorporate at least one activity that builds spelling and vocabulary skills.

Step Seven: Make It Fun

You don't have to be a kid to appreciate fun. Learning is always easier when it is presented in a playful way. Each learner is an individual with her own unique learning style. Our mission as literacy leaders is to present the same concept in multiple forms until one sticks. This is where the literacy leader's creativity takes the lead. How many ways can you think of presenting "silent e" words until this idea clicks for the learner?

Much of reading is grounded in sound, but also it is important to integrate visual and tactile activities. I often use a sand tray with clients who have trouble remembering the sounds of the letters. For example, they draw each letter in the sand as they say, "'A' sounds like "ah" and "ay." Forming words with word tiles or letter stamps are another great tactile way to work on spelling.

My favorite visual exercise involves an art book I composed, filled with postcards I've collected from art museums and travel adventures. The learner flips through the book until an image strikes him in some way. Then I give him a writing prompt, usually relating to the specific image, like, "Write a story that describes the conversation you imagine is happening in that painting."

Other fun activities include dictating a story to the client to write, Choose Your News, Word Finds, Letter To My Younger Self, and Loco Logos. See Chapter 11 for the full Literacy Kit.

Step 7 of a successful literacy session incorporates fun activities that include audio, visual, and tactile exercises.

Staying on Track

Before each session

o Have a lesson planned with activities from Chapter 11, a writing exercise, and backup workbook pages.

During each session

o Check in with the learner. How is he doing? Is there anything occupying his mind? If so, improvise and use that issue to build your lesson upon. Rapport is the most important component of the session. Often real life matters can influence what is covered in the session and we can use those issues to bridge what the learner wants to learn with what we're teaching in a literacy session.

o Review what was covered last week with the learner to build confidence and motivate the learner about what will be covered next. Positive encouragement goes a long way. We are building bridges between what is already known with what is unknown.

o Reading. The learner should complete a reading activity, whether it's from the workbook or from another source, such as a newspaper or book of poetry.

o Writing. The client should compose a story or a written response to a reading. Writing prompts can be in the form of a question and they can be image-inspired. These writing exercises are used to build their writing portfolio, which we use for progress assessment and as a springboard for issues to be addressed. Instead of correcting the page, start a new page with follow-up exercises that address spelling or grammatical problems found in the writing sample. The writing sample should be praised and used to motivate and encourage the learner rather than as a reminder that they have much more work to do. Otherwise they will begin to dread this part of the session.

o   Encourage the learner to make decisions in the session. Offer a selection of fun activities (Chapter 11) that the learner may choose from.

o   End each session with a new Weekly Reading Log and a summary of what the learner hopes to learn next week (short-term goals). Find out if there's something specific that the learner wants to address in next week's session so that it can be prepared ahead of time. Example: if the learner needs help with a job application or DMV form this could be an activity included in the next session.

After each session

o   Summarize what was covered in the session and any observations about the learner's progress or areas for improvement in a Teaching Log. This helps you further document the progress and prepare for next week's session.

Chapter 11
Literacy Kit

"We have a hunger of the mind. We ask for all of the knowledge around us and the more we get, the more we desire." –Maria Mitchell

This chapter offers 50 activities in reading, writing, health, numeracy, and digital literacy, to help make your literacy sessions hands-on, fun, relevant to life and learner-centered.

Real Life Literacy Goals Checklist

_____ Know the letters and sounds of each letter in the alphabet
_____ Read a subway map
_____ Write name and address
_____ Complete a job application
_____ Complete an online job application
_____ Identify and understand key safety words
_____ Compose a cover letter
_____ Read and comprehend job ads
_____ Create a job-appropriate email address
_____ Send at least five email messages
_____ Attach documents, like a resume, to an email
_____ Use a dictionary
_____ Write a check
_____ Understand a paystub
_____ Balance a checkbook
_____ Create a budget
_____ Tell time
_____ Read a calendar

_____ Read and understand a New Employee Manual
_____ Read and understand prescription dosage directions

Flashy Flashcards

Whether the learner is mastering vowel sounds or is building up his word bank, creating flashcards can be a fun activity that builds rapport and connects creativity with new knowledge.

Supplies:

o   Index cards
o   Old magazines or images printed from the Internet
o   Glitter, beads, sequins, stickers, and any other craft material
o   Glue
o   Markers

First, identify which words or concepts you will be creating flashcards for. Make a list of problem letters or words and make only a few flash cards at a time. Gather old magazines or materials printed from the Internet.

The learner should decide which words to tackle first and making an art project out of creating flashcards provides another way to connect the word with its meaning and offers a visual and tactile approach.

Flashcards are helpful for review during the literacy session and they also serve as a good teaching tool to send home with the learner.

Loco Logos

Learners have a number of words that they recognize by sight, meaning they are memorized. Many of these words are logos or slogans from advertisements. Learners will know the names of fast food restaurants, sports teams, or favorite sodas, without even knowing how to sound out words. They will see the red and white logo of the store Target and be able to say, "target." This exercise builds from what is already familiar to the learner and connects new words with ones they are already familiar with.

Using magazines, newspapers, or the print outs from the Internet, cut out logos that have both the logo and the word for the company or brand. Paste them onto a piece of paper. Present these logos to the learner and see which ones she recognizes by sight.

Build words and sentences together from the logos the learner recognizes. For instance, if "Target" is one that the learner recognizes, use each letter or sound unit in Target to connect to other words that the learner is working on. Target is a great word to connect with other words that also have the sound "ar." Words like "large, far, market, car," would be great.

1) Review the sounds that make up the brand name.
2) With the learner, come up with other words that have similar sounds and spellings.
3) Create sentences with those words. Come up with a sentence that the learner can complete by identifying and correctly spelling the missing word.

Poem of The Day

Poems are a useful teaching tool because they tend to be shorter than other written material and rhythm and sound are important to all poems, even in non-rhyming poems. This is another way of connecting what the learner hears with how things look when they are written.

I always begin every new literacy relationship by reading Langston Hughes's great poem, "Hold Fast To Dreams." I like this poem because it highlights the importance of goals and holding onto our dreams. No matter what barriers we may face, we always have our dreams and no one can take those away from us. Holding onto our dreams and working towards them is what gives us power.

The rhyming of the poem makes it easier to read and to discern whether the learner can identify the rhyming words. If he can't, it teaches me that this will be something to work towards. Even if the learner is not at the level to read the poem aloud on his own, pointing to each word as you read it out loud to the learner is just as useful and listening to a poem or story and then discussing its meaning is always a good exercise to build reading comprehension skills.

Here is a list of recommended poems:

o "Hold Fast To Dreams," by Langston Hughes
o "Still I Rise," by Maya Angelou
o "Immigrants In Our Own Land" and "Painters" and "So Mexicans Are Taking Jobs From Americans," or really anything by Jimmy Santiago Baca
o "We Real Cool," by Gwendolyn Brooks
o "Happiness," by Raymond Carver
o "I Hear America Singing," by Walt Whitman
o "Forgetfulness," by Billie Collins
o "The Road Not Taken," by Robert Frost
o "The Great Figure" and "Hurricane," by William Carlos Williams
o "If" by Rudyard Kipling
o "Lilacs in September," by Katha Pollitt
o "Public Transportation," by Elaine Sexton
o "We Wear The Mask" by Paul Laurence Dunbar

o "I Am Much Too Alone In This World, Yet Not Alone," by Rainer Maria Rilke
o "Grief Calls Us to the Things of This World," by Sherman Alexie
o "The Dead Woman," by Pablo Neruda
o "Quilts," by Nikki Giovanni

Socially Relevant Stories & Resources

The following is a list of recommended reading based on most requested, favorites of clients, and a few others that I thought would be helpful for the literacy leader. Most are best suited for learners who have reached the GED level. Sometimes learners who are not at that level yet will request a work from this list and in that case I present a page or two of the work and let them know it will become much easier with time. Let the learner decide for himself if he is ready to take it on. Let him know it's fine to read just one sentence or one paragraph and come back to it later when he is ready. Take turns reading passages to each other and make sure you point to the words as you read.

Even if the learner has reached the GED level, I recommend introducing just a few pages at a time, and only add more if the learner seems enthusiastic about continuing the story. There are many other great socially relevant works, but these are some favorites of learners I've worked with.

o *The Change Agent, An Adult Education Newspaper For Social Justice* is a revolutionary resource that highlights how current events are directly relevant and important. Their website (http://www.nelrc.org/changeagent/) also offers activities and submission opportunities for learners and educators.
o *The Week*, a weekly magazine of current events

- *A Place To Stand* by Jimmy Santiago Baca
- "Sonny's Blues" by James Baldwin
- "Outlaw," by Jose Antonio Vargas, *The New York Times Magazine*, June 26, 2011
- "Girl," by Jamaica Kincaid
- "The Money," by Junot Diaz, *The New Yorker,* June 13 & 20, 2011
- "Where I'm Calling From" by Raymond Carver
- "Beverly Home," from *Jesus' Son* by Denis Johnson
- "Black Dog," by Walter Mosley
- "Reverting To A Wild State" by Justin Torres, *The New Yorker*, August 1, 2011
- *War Dances* by Sherman Alexie
- *The Lone Ranger and Tonto Fistfight In Heaven*, by Sherman Alexie
- *Jesus Hopped The A Train,* a play by Stephen Adly Guirgis
- *The Exonerated*, a play by Jessica Blank and Erik Jensen
- *A People's History of The United States* by Howard Zinn
- *Beloved* by Toni Morrison
- *Naked* by David Sedaris
- *The Autobiography of Malcom X: As Told to Alex Haley*
- *Invisible Man* by Ralph Ellison
- *Native Son* by Richard Wright
- *The New Jim Crow* by Michelle Alexander
- *Fire In The Ashes: Twenty-Five Years Among the Poorest Children in America* by Jonathan Kozol
- *One Size Does Not Fit All: A Student's Assessment of School* by Nikhil Goyal
- *The Readers' Advisory Guide To Street Literature* by Vanessa Irvin Morris is a helpful guide for educators that lists many book titles for teens and adults.

Spot The Scam

Spot The Scam is real life application of reading comprehension and critical thinking skills.

Unfortunately, many people still operate under the impression that if something is in print, even if they can't read the words, it is true. It would be nice if everything printed were true and companies only sold products that were good for our consumption, good for the environment, etc., but this is not the case. We live in a time when critical thinking is imperative to survival. We must question everything.

In order to teach this skill, it is helpful to show examples of both legitimate materials as well as examples of scams or fraud. Make a game out of identifying which ones are legit and which ones are scams. Discussing WHY something is a fraud or WHY it seems legit is an integral part of this activity.

The next time you receive an email from the Prince of Nairobi offering you millions of dollars, print out a copy before deleting it. Go on Craigslist.org and print out two or three job ads from "General Labor" and "Security." At least one of the ads should be one that seems it is probably legitimate and one should definitely be a scam. The scams are the ones that offer a ridiculously high hourly wage for an entry-level job, cell phone numbers instead of business phone numbers, are often written in all caps, and try too hard to get the reader's attention. If it seems too good to be true, it is.

For the examples that are not scams, discuss how one would go about applying to the job and what makes it different from the others.

While this activity is great for building critical thinking skills, always remind the learner that it isn't the end of the world if he accidentally sends his resume to a scammer. The object is to show the learner how to navigate the Internet and the world without fear. Fear often stems from what is unknown. Teaching about fraud and how to avoid being scammed should be empowering and shouldn't create more fear. As long as the learner doesn't reveal her social security number and date of birth on her resume, there's really no harm done, if she accidentally sends her resume to a scammer.

Weird News

When learners begin reading the newspaper each day their reading improves at a much faster rate. News stories provide information about day-to-day life stories that are directly relevant to all of our lives. Staying on top of current events is important for any member of society, and for adult and teen learners, connecting with the news builds confidence and reinforces why literacy matters.

Sometimes learners are reluctant to read the news, and especially if they are struggling with an issue like recovery, they will often have an aversion to thinking about things that carry a negative message, which almost all news stories do. Be sensitive to this when you're selecting news stories.

I highly recommend perusing the "Weird News" section of *The San Francisco Chronicle* (http://www.sfgate.com/weird/). This section offers a collection of the funniest and bizarre news stories from all over the world and is updated daily. Stories are often short and use simple language, perfect material for a literacy session.

Another great source of news material is the weekly news magazine called *The Week*. This publication offers a news summary of stories all over the world, but with a focus on the United States. It also offers a plethora of odd news stories, each only a few sentences long. Also, *The Week* offers excerpts from editorials from all over the world, which are good to use as examples or starting points if you're working with the learner on how to write a GED essay.

Whatever source material you choose, here are the steps that you should incorporate into your literacy session:

1) Have the learner read the story out loud.
2) Review any difficult words by identifying them and offering similar words that may have similar sounds or spellings.
3) Ask two or three questions relating to the story to make sure the learner understood what was happening in the story.
4) Have the learner write a short story (it can be a paragraph) somehow relating to the news story. Perhaps the story reminded the learner of another story. Or create a brand new story by using a character in the news story or a theme presented in the news story.

Safety Word List

o **Caution**: *noun*, a warning of danger
o **Danger**: *noun*, risk of harm
o **Injury**: *noun*, physical or psychological harm that is done
o **Injuries**: *plural noun*, more than one injury
o **Flammable**: *adjective,* easily set on fire
o **Inflammable**: *adjective*, not easily set on fire
o **Combustible**: *adjective*, will easily catch on fire
o **Poisonous**: *adjective*, containing poison and very harmful
o **Corrosive**: *adjective,* having the ability to eat away or destroy

- **Emergency**: *noun*, a sudden crisis that requires immediate action
- **Do Not Mix**: instructions to avoid combining two or more items
- **Avoid**: *verb*, keep away from
- **Prohibit**: *verb,* to forbid
- **Permit**: *verb*, to allow
- **Required**: *verb*, must do something
- **Safety**: *noun*, freedom from the risk of danger
- **Equipment**: *noun*, tools, machinery, anything kept for a specific purpose
- **Regulations**: *plural noun*, rules
- **Risk**: *noun,* the chance of injury or danger; *verb*: to take or run the chance of loss "to risk one's life"
- **Hazard**: *noun*, an unavoidable danger
- **Hazardous** *adjective*, full of danger
- **Bleach**: *noun*, a chemical used to lighten a stain or clean. Never mix with ammonia.
- **Ammonia**: *noun*, a chemical used to clean. Never mix with bleach.
- **First Aid Kit**: *noun*, emergency treatment supplies to use for a medical crisis before the medical professionals arrive
- **Emergency Kit**: *noun*, another term for First Aid Kit
- **Warning**: *noun,* something that gives a notice of caution
- **Evacuate**: *verb*, to leave or vacate
- **First Responder**: *noun,* a person who is certified to provide medical care in emergencies until a more highly trained team arrives
- **EMT**: *noun,* stands for Emergency Medical Technician, a person who is trained and certified to treat medical emergencies at the scene of the crisis
- **CPR**: *noun,* stands for cardiopulmonary resuscitation, an emergency treatment to revive heart and lung function
- **911**: *noun,* the number to call when there is an emergency situation

Job Application Word List

o **Maintenance**: *noun,* the act of maintaining care or upkeep
o **Full-time**: *noun*, working 40 hours per week
o **Diploma**: *noun*, certificate of achievement
o **Certificate**: *noun*, document of achievement
o **Employer**: *noun*, the company that you work for
o **Supervisor**: *noun*, the boss
o **Former**: *adjective*, prior, earlier, preceding in time
o **Opportunity**: *noun*, a favorable occurrence or event
o **Honor**: *noun*, integrity or high respect or worth
o **Privilege**: *noun*, a benefit enjoyed by a person beyond the advantages of most
o **Knowledge**: *noun*, the act of knowing facts or truths
o **Position**: *noun*, place or situation
o **Responding**: *verb*, to reply
o **Sincerely**: *adjective*, the act of being sincere or earnest
o **Negotiate**: *verb*, to make a deal
o **Negotiable**: *adjective*, able to be negotiated
o **Benefit**: *noun*, something extra that is good
o **Benefit***: verb*, to do something good
o **Salary requirements**: *noun*, the salary that is needed
o **Unfortunate**: *adjective*, regrettable
o **Rehabilitate**: *verb,* to return to a good condition
o **Acquire**: *verb*, to obtain or get
o **Achievement**: *noun*, something accomplished
o **Procure**: *verb*, to obtain or get
o **Background***: noun*, the historical information about something
o **Believe**: *verb*, to have confidence in a belief
o **Restaurant**: *noun,* an establishment where meals are served

Word Bank

Encourage the learner to keep a notebook with her at all times in order to jot down unfamiliar words.

These words may come up in conversation, in ads, a newspaper, or on the job.

Each time when you meet with the learner, ask what new words she has found that week. Bring a dictionary to your sessions and show her how to look up unfamiliar words and demonstrate how to read the phonetic breakdown of each word. Have the learner write down the correct spelling and definition of each new word.

Spelling quizzes are a good activity to include in your sessions each week, especially if you are drawing from words in the learner's Word Bank or from the Safety Word List and Job Application Word List. This keeps the progress focused and gives the learner a chance to study words that are relevant to life, which will make a longer lasting impact on the learner's memory and ability to connect new ideas with familiar ones.

Gradually, the learner's Word Bank will grow and looking back on words she has mastered over time should bring a feeling of accomplishment.

Journal

Encourage the learner to keep a journal. This journal can be a collection of Word Bank words or it can be a place to list goals or vent frustrations. If the learner is still working on how to build sentences, encourage her to compile a list of study words and perhaps paste pictures from magazines and newspapers, which can also hold similar meanings for the learner as she processes the events of the day and plans for the future.

Joke Book

Everyone likes to laugh. Puns and jokes are a great way to make reading and word study fun. I once bought a children's joke book for a learner who had two kids in elementary school. We read the book together and went over difficult words, adding a few of them to our word bank along the way.

I found that puns offered a new way of discussing sound and spelling and just how strange the English language can be with all of its rule exceptions.

For instance, take this joke told to me by Vanessa Lozano, a good friend and teacher of ESOL and literacy:

"Why didn't the peanut want to go back to New York?"

"He was assaulted."

Obviously, this joke is a play on the words "salted" and "assaulted." With this joke we discussed how both words have similar sounds but have two different spellings and meanings.

The learner was able to go over these bad jokes with his kids and seemed to really get a kick out of doing so.

Song Lyrics

Everyone appreciates music and no matter the genre, rhythm is absolutely essential. One of the first things I usually ask my clients is what kind of music they like and who are some of their favorite artists. This helps build rapport and it will help you plan this activity.

1) Ask the learner to name a few of his favorite songs.
2) Either with the learner or before the next session: look up the lyrics on the Internet. Print them out.

3) Play the song and ask the learner to read as he listens to the song.
4) After the song is over, read some or all of the lines out loud and discuss the song's rhythm and any rhymes.
5) Encourage the learner to tell you about more songs and over time you will compose a book of song lyrics that the learner can read as he listens to his favorite songs. This helps the learner visualize the spelling of words with how they sound. This connection between image and sound are imperative to building literacy skills.

Music artists often take liberties with spellings and shorten words. Definitely point this out when you are reading the lyrics out loud and spell out for the learner the word that the artist has abbreviated so he can see the difference.

Sand Tray Play

This activity works best with learners who are still mastering the sounds of each letter. Often we have to backtrack and review the sounds of each individual letter before we can effectively blend two or more sounds together.

Say the name and its sound as you draw the letter with your finger in the sand tray. "A says ah," and "A says ay." After you demonstrate for the learner, have the learner try practicing this tactile and repetitious exercise for each of the letter that is challenging the learner.

Composing Words With Letter Tiles

Build words and sentences with letter tiles. This is a tactile and fun way of working on spelling skills, utilizing the learner's imagination, phonetic reasoning, and memory.

Pour several tiles on the table and ask the learner how many words he can form. If the learner is more advanced, create sentences and discuss where punctuation marks would be placed.

Stamp Art

To mix it up and shift the focus from handwriting, I recommend investing in rubber stamps of each letter and an inkpad. This is a more playful way for the learner to work on spelling skills without feeling self-conscious about handwriting. Create holiday or birthday cards for loved ones, posters, or just do spelling drills using rubber stamps.

Word Finds

Pick up a booklet of word finds at your local drugstore. Word finds offer a fun warm up exercise or homework exercise. Searching for words in Word Finds reinforces the learner's spelling and word recognition skills.

Choose Your News

Take an article out of the newspaper and type up a shorter, simpler version. Omit certain words. A headline that was "Shark Attack On The Northern Coast," could be "_____ Attack On The Northern _____."

You can either show the learner the story with the missing words and ask the learner to fill in the blank or you can ask the learner to brainstorm a number of words that will be filled in later. The story will be much funnier if the learner doesn't know the context.

Robyn's Fill-It-In Game

This activity is named after Robyn Olds, an artist with whom I had the privilege of teaching. She invented this activity and used it while working with her literacy clients.

Using words from the learner's life, such as Job Application Word List or the Safety Word List, write an underline dash for each letter of the word and offer one or two letters to help the learner get started. For instance, "maintain," might look like this, "_ a _ n t _ _ _"

This activity makes a game out of spelling and is less daunting than putting the learner on the spot and asking him to spell the entire word without any clues.

Sentence or Fragment?

Sometimes I do this activity following the Poem of the Day activity and point out that poems are usually composed of fragments. With the learner, create a fragment, like "ran around the house." Then ask how he would change it into a sentence and rewrite it as a complete sentence. For instance, it could be changed to, "Larry ran around the house," or "Larry ran around the house trying to find the mouse."

Or, create a few sentence fragments and complete sentences and ask the learner to identify which are fragments and which are sentences.

Discuss why it is a sentence or not.

To review, every sentence has an action word (a verb) and a subject (a noun) and completes a thought. The easiest way to dissect a sentence is to begin with identifying the action or the verb. Let's look at the sentence, "John ran the office for five years." First, we identify the verb, which is "ran." Then we ask who or what "ran?" The answer is "John." So John is our subject and "the office for five years" completes the thought.

Using a newspaper or book ask the learner to pick out a simple sentence, and practice identifying the verbs and subjects. Then ask the learner to create a sentence on his own.

Marketing Yourself

Literacy is not just the ability to read and write well, it is also the ability to speak and communicate effectively. Whether the learner is job-searching or working towards a promotion at her current job, role-playing and practicing answers that market the learner's strengths are the first steps toward success. The book, *Good In A Room*, by Stephanie Palmer, and Harvey Semler, a great job developer with whom I used to work inspired this activity.

The concept of an elevator pitch started in Hollywood when an ambitious newcomer would luck into finding himself in an elevator with a film production executive and have only a few seconds to peak the exec's interest in a project. We may not live in Hollywood, but often what we are trying to get has even higher stakes than the next blockbuster movie. We are trying to land jobs so that we can feed our children or promotions so that we can adjust to cost inflation.

The key to marketing one's self is confidence. Confidence is directly related to being prepared, which is why it's important to create a solid and concise answer and then rehearse it. With the learner, you can develop a series of pitches based on the learner's needs and upcoming issues, whether she is trying to secure employment, or describe how she's changed and shouldn't be discriminated against because of a criminal conviction in her background, or why she deserves the promotion at work.

Ask the learner to try to market himself in a couple of sentences. The pitch should be relevant to the task at hand and it should be concise. If he is preparing for a job interview, practice some commonly asked interview answers with him. Help the learner brainstorm and write down his pitch, and finally, rehearse.

Here are three examples:

1) *Job Interview/Tell me about yourself*: "I am a custodial maintenance expert with over ten years of experience working in both indoor environments, such as offices and restaurants, and outdoor settings, including large public events like New Year's Eve in Manhattan. I am known for being a hard-working perfectionist with excellent customer service skills."

2) *Asking for a promotion*: "I have enjoyed serving you and my maintenance team over the past year. In that time, I have collected a number of excellent service reports from our customers, I've never missed a day of work, I've taken on more responsibilities, like opening and closing the store, and I now have a GED. For those reasons, I hope you will consider my application for the store manager position. It would be an honor to continue expanding my career under your supervision."

3) *Job Interview/Describing conviction history*: Yes, unfortunately, I made a mistake many years ago and have a non-violent, non-theft felony on my record. But I have changed a lot since then. I have been clean and sober for eight years, volunteer at my local community center, and have helped to raise two of my children as well as my sister's children. I am known as a mentor in my community and love working with people, which is why I am especially excited about the receptionist position with your company.

Health Literacy

It has been reported by University of California, San Francisco author Dr. Dean Schillinger, that nearly half of the US population has difficulty understanding medical instructions and making informed decisions about their healthcare. Understanding dosage instructions could mean the difference between life and death.

Find out if the learner has any medical issues that he may need help with. Medical forms and instructions are difficult to read. What prescriptions does he take each day? Does he understand when he is to take the medicine and how much each time?

Does the learner understand what to do in an emergency situation? Review how the learner would dial 911 and help him write down and program his primary doctor's phone number and that of his children's in his diary and in his cell phone.

Search for your state's Patient's Bill of Rights and review them with the learner. Most will state the importance of asking questions of the health care provider and the patient's right to understand his treatment. Hospitals cannot refuse to treat patients based on their lack of health insurance. This is an important right that everyone should be aware of and enforced.

Planning for worst case scenarios and being prepared for traumatic events before they arise will alleviate stress and will remove what could be a fatal hurdle for the learner.

Grocery List

Part of living well is making smart choices about the foods we consume. Just because the learner may be living on food stamps or a limited budget does not mean that she must resort to liquor store food shopping, where foods are high in starch and corn syrup, not to mention overpriced.

Discuss the food groups and any special dietary needs or allergies that exist for the learner and her family. Create a menu of meals that are balanced and nutritious and discuss which ingredients would be required. Discuss how planning well can save money, where leftovers are incorporated into new healthy meals. For instance, when my husband roasts a chicken, he uses the whole bird throughout the week in sandwiches, fettuccine, and chicken soup.

Make a list of groceries and their approximate costs. How does this fit in with the budget she has already established? Are there items that she could cut down on or increase? Be sure to tie in the numeracy (budget and fractions) component with the health component.

There is a common misconception that it costs more to eat well. While this can be true when it comes to exclusively purchasing organic foods from big chain grocery stores, there is a way to locate produce sellers that offer produce from local farms and are less expensive than gourmet stores. To further solidify the concept of saving money and eating well, discuss how she may be able to use the extra money that will be left over.

Calendar

Organization can make the difference between keeping your job and losing your job, this skill can help a person pick up their kids on time and be able to balance work, family, and all of life's obligations with ease.

Does the learner already have a system in place for staying organized? If so, are there any areas that need improvement?

Discuss how you stay organized with the learner. Do you use an electronic calendar or an old school hard copy calendar or both? What would the learner prefer to use? How does making a To Do list help a person stay organized? Show the learner how to make a To Do list and how to incorporate this into a weekly or monthly calendar.

Discuss how planning ahead can alleviate stress and build confidence as the learner stays on top of his game.

Letter to My Younger Self

The Last Word section of the December 9, 2011 issue of *The Week* inspired this activity. Several celebrity writers and film stars wrote letters to themselves. Some were lighthearted and witty, while others had a more serious tone.

If you could write a letter to your teenaged self, now that you are a wise adult, what advice would you give yourself? Would you recommend studying more or avoid getting into certain relationships or buying stock in Google? Or if the learner is a teenager, what would she write to her little kid self? This reflective exercise can be used to build the learner's writing portfolio and is a positive reminder that change is an important and empowering part of life.

Journal of My Future Self

This activity imagines that the learner's goals have been actualized. Imagining is the first step to becoming. Ask the learner to imagine himself five or ten years from now. Where is he living? What does he do for a living? Who are the important people in his life? This is a journal entry of the future. The learner has already become the person he wishes to be and now he is describing a day in his life. Perhaps it is a birthday, or the day he graduates from college, or the birthday of his grandchild, but it should describe what his life is like and how he has already reached some of his goals.

Trigger This

Many of the learners I have worked with were in recovery from substance abuse. They often spoke of moments of triumph and relapse. An important part of relapse prevention is being able to identify your triggers, the "people, places, or things," that can lead to relapse.

If the learner is in recovery and feels comfortable discussing this with you, it can be helpful for the learner to write about moments when he has been able to overcome some of his triggers. Ask him to write a story about when he exhibited the courage to not give in to one of his triggers.

It is important to frame this exercise in a positive way. Don't ask the learner to write about a recent relapse because recalling the traumatic event could serve as a trigger and lead to another relapse.

This exercise should be focused in building confidence and supporting the learner in his journey to overcome addiction.

Create a Visual Writing Prompt Book

I collect postcards from places and museums I've visited over the years and I compiled them in a portfolio. Some are photographs of actual places or people, some are abstract splashes of colors, and some are realist paintings of a specific setting.

I recommend creating your own collection of postcards and ask the learner to flip through the book until an image speaks to her or grabs her interest in some way. Ask her to then write a story about the image, what she imagined happened right before the photograph was taken or what she imagines the characters in the painting are saying to each other. Help her get started by asking her to write from a certain perspective. Offer some parameters based on the image she's chosen.

Be sure to mark the date on this writing exercise so you can include it in the learner's writing portfolio.

Story Dictation

Writing is often a difficult task for learners who are still mastering their reading skills. This activity builds confidence and helps the learner make connections between the audio and visual aspects of words and sentences.

Explain to the learner that together you are going to write a story. It can be a true story or not, but take the pressure off the learner by telling him that he won't have to write it down. Give the learner a topic or ask him to tell you about a time when he laughed the hardest.

You will write the story as the learner speaks it. Then you will read it aloud to the learner. Discuss where you placed periods and commas and other punctuation marks and why. Point out how most letters were lowercase and remind the learner of when capital letters are used. Ask if the spelling of any of the words surprised the learner. Compliment the story. Emphasize how it was his story - he created it. Then ask the learner to read the story to you.

Another way to do this activity is to reverse roles. If the learner is able to write some words and you have already established a strong rapport, dictate a few very simple sentences to the learner, who will write them down.

It is important to go slow and only tackle one sentence at a time rather than making him write a paragraph before offering corrections. The aim of this exercise is to build confidence and strengthen spelling and grammar skills, not make the learner feel overwhelmed.

Group Story

This activity is similar to Story Dictation, except that you and the learner create a story together. One person writes a sentence and then the other builds from that sentence and creates a new one. The story is constructed sentence by sentence.

Address spelling and grammar issues as they arise. This activity builds comprehension as well as spelling and grammar skills because the learner will have to logically connect what has been written with what he will write.

Poetry Collage

This is an artful way of using words from the learner's Word Bank. Poetry, whether it consists of rhyming lines or not, is usually written in fragments. This removes grammar from the focus of constructing meaning from language and allows the learner to focus on syllables, phonemic awareness, spelling, and meaning.

Ask the learner to create a collage of words, drawing from the learner's Word Bank, lines from favorite songs, bits of overheard conversations, or lines borrowed from the news.

To inspire the learner, start this activity by reading a poem from the Poem of the Day list or another poem that you and the learner enjoy.

Ghost Story

It doesn't have to be a ghost story, but I've always enjoyed this exercise more when it is one. The main idea is to give the learner a good beginning to a story from which to work. Give the learner a writing prompt and ask him to do a free write for ten minutes. Encourage him to be as creative as possible. This is a good activity to help build the learner's writing portfolio, which provides a qualitative example of progress.

Make corrections on a separate page so that the learner does not form a negative association between writing exercises and criticism. Remember, that this is literacy triage and the aim is not to create perfect literature, but to address one hurdle at a time, while building the learner's confidence.

Here are some writing prompts:

o The old house had been abandoned for twenty-five years, until one day…
o Everyone knows the park behind the high school is haunted, but I
o Beth was the last one to see her boss alive.
o Mark had never been afraid of anything, until the night he was locked out of…
o Most nights they were awoken by a loud thumping sound, coming from the…
o Years later she would look back and realize her dream may have been a premonition.

A Happy Ending

In this writing exercise, the ending of the story has been provided for the learner and he must imagine a series of events that culminate with the story ending that way. Here are some endings:

o And that was how I got away with the trunk full of cash.
o Finally, we found him waiting for us back at the house, safe and fast asleep.
o That's why I have decided to not tell anyone the next time I win the lottery.
o In the end, it's really just those special moments spent with family that matter.
o I may still be a kid, but I've learned how to plan for the future and stay ahead of the game.
o We boarded the plane as the sun began to set.

How to Write a GED Essay

If the learner has not already earned a high school diploma or a GED, then it should certainly be a goal that she is working towards. This significant piece of paper can increase the learner's annual earnings by thousands of dollars, not to mention the self-esteem boost. This activity takes a few sessions to complete.

There is no shortage of GED workbooks that can help prepare teens or adults for the GED, but learners who are building literacy skills need a lot of catching up before they are ready for GED-level material. It's always a good idea to remind the learner why literacy is important and how reading, writing, and speaking well can directly impact life choices and even salary.

Start planning for the GED by demystifying the GED essay, which is usually the biggest hurdle for clients who are catching up their literacy skills. Much of the challenge is the psychological block that the learner has developed about this part of the test. By simplifying and practicing the steps, the learner will overcome these internal barriers while also continuing to build literacy skills. Here is a way to break it down into manageable pieces:

1) What is an essay? An essay is a written composition that makes an argument or expresses the author's opinion. This should be fun, right? Everyone has opinions. Offer some examples of essay questions.

   – Do you think reading is important for children to learn?
   – What is your dream vacation?
   – Do you think parenting skills are learned from our parents or instinctual?

  – If you were appointed leader of the world tomorrow, what would be the first thing you would change?
  – Do you think compassion is a trait inherent to all people or is it learned?

Explore the learner's immediate gut reaction to the questions through simple conversation.

2) The learner will have 45 minutes to compose an essay and the very first step is actually the most important and is often skipped due to sheer panic. As soon as the learner reads the essay prompt, he should take about two minutes and brainstorm, listing the first thoughts that come to mind as he considers the question. Help the learner decide whether he prefers to brainstorm in a list form or a web form by trying both. Then practice organizing the reasons and thoughts so that when he begins the actual writing of the essay, his thoughts will be coherent and flow in a logical manner.

3) The GED essay is only five paragraphs. It's not a book and it's not a research paper. It is a composition of the learner's opinion in five paragraphs. This is a good time to talk about what constitutes a paragraph and a sentence. Each paragraph should have three to five sentences.

4) Find a couple of sample GED essays on the Internet and read them with the learner. Does he notice the structural formula? All GED essays are structured this way:

Paragraph 1: Introduces the essay topic and offers a general argument or opinion, while allowing room for the supporting paragraphs to delve more specifically into each reason. The introduction restates the question as a declarative sentence.

Paragraphs 2, 3, & 4: The body of the GED essay. These paragraphs should describe the reasons why the author thinks whatever she thinks.

These are specific reasons that should logically flow with the rest of the essay and get into the heart of the argument.

Paragraph 5: Concludes the essay. This paragraph summarizes everything that was just written, but in three to five sentences.

5) Revise. After the learner has written a first draft, it is important that he read what has been written and rewrite it so that it has fewer errors and reads even better than it did the first time.

How to Write a Cover Letter

The cover letter is the first impression and should concisely relate the learner's relevant work experience to the job for which he is applying. It should contain no spelling or grammatical errors. The purpose is to grab the employer's attention and make her want to look at the resume.

Most communication is made via email and does not need to include the employer's address and the date. For an emailed cover letter, the letter should be typed or pasted into the body of the email.

1) It begins with Dear Mr./Ms. First Name Last Name or "To Whom It May Concern:" if the prospective employer's name is unknown.

2) The first sentence should state that the learner is writing to apply for the job and be sure to name the position title. Follow this sentence with a pitch or one sentence summary of your work experience and how it relates to the job at hand. For instance, "I am a licensed plumber and my background offers over ten years of plumbing and building maintenance experience."

3) The second paragraph should summarize the experience listed in the resume and how it directly relates to the job ad. It's a good idea to use similar language as found in the job ad.
4) The third paragraph restates with enthusiasm how this is the dream job of the learner's life and states that he appreciates the prospective employer's time and consideration.
5) The closing is "Sincerely," and don't forget the comma.
6) The learner's name.

I recommend perusing cover letter samples and resumes from the Internet and review this formula with the learner before creating one together.

Revising and Reviewing The Resume

The resume tells a story and is a marketing tool for the learner. It is a document that should entice prospective employers into calling the learner for an interview. It must be accurate and honest, but also it should help the learner stand out from other candidates.

1) Show the learner the standard format by offering your own resume or others from the Internet.
2) The basic information should include the learner's name and contact info at the very top and a list of jobs that describe experience starting with bullet point action words (verbs) that are past tense if the learner is no longer employed there or present tense if he still works there.
3) It's a good idea to mention that the learner is pursuing his GED at the end, under Education, if he has that as a goal. Adult learners who return to school can increase their annual salary by thousands of dollars when they earn their GED.

4) Gaps in the resume can be remedied by listing productive activities the learner accomplished during periods of unemployment or incarceration, even if he was not paid for his work. For instance, if he helped take care of his family during that time, this could be listed as "Caretaker" with the responsibilities described in the same manner as actual jobs. If he was incarcerated, but earned a certificate in maintenance during that time or had cooking responsibilities, these should certainly be included. Experience is experience, even if the person wasn't paid for the services. See the "Marketing Yourself" exercise for an example of how to describe a past conviction during a job interview, which will hopefully someday be illegal for employers to ask.

Completing a Winning Job Application

This activity is a good real life way for the learner to put into practice the Job Application Word List she has been building and a way to review sentence structure, grammar, and how to market herself in a way that is concise and correct.

1) Collect job applications from local shops or use one from the Internet.
2) Ask the learner to bring a copy of her resume. Make sure the cell phone number is still current. Review all of the other information that is listed on it, especially the fact that each job is listed in reverse chronological order, which is the same order that jobs will be listed on the application.

3) After you have reviewed the resume, ask the learner to begin completing the application. It's best to do these exercises in pencil, so the learner may easily erase mistakes. I have noticed over time that many learners have difficulty writing everything from their address to even their phone numbers, putting "1" before each phone number or grouping numbers in random clusters rather than groups of three and four.

4) The object of this exercise is to create an impeccable application by addressing mistakes as they arise. Depending on the level of functioning, do not expect this activity to be completed in one session. It's best to do a little bit each time and break this activity up by offering other activities in between, so the learner does not get frustrated.

5) Once you and the learner have successfully completed an error-free application, make a photocopy of it so the learner may take it with her when she applies for work, as a cheat sheet of sorts.

6) Practice makes perfect. This is a good activity to repeat with the learner so she won't make embarrassing mistakes when she actually needs to apply for a job.

Following Up

Following up is an important skill, especially now when we are constantly bombarded with so much information and expected to be available 24/7 on cell phones and email. We need a lot of reminding and for this reason it is imperative to follow-up with others after important meetings or events, such as job interviews, meetings with your son's school principal, the probation officer.

What upcoming events might she want to follow up with a thank you note? Practice writing thank you notes on paper or via email with the learner. Here is an example:

Dear Mr. Tom Jazzplayer,

Thank you for taking the time to meet with me today. I am very excited about the Retail Associate position.

It would be an honor to serve Tom's Turntables & Typewriters Emporium. I appreciate your consideration.

Sincerely,

Sam Soccerstar

Maps & Directions

One of my clients was very eager and motivated to find a job and finally got an interview, but when he tried to get to there, he took the downtown train instead of the uptown train and missed his appointment.

He is not alone. Many people do not have a sense of direction or even understand the basic concept of North, East, South, and West.

The best way to address this problem is to work with a local map and present scenarios to the learner in which he is starting in one place and must get to the next.

1) Print out or purchase a local map. Try to get one that is printed in larger print so that it will seem less crowded and overwhelming to the learner.

2) On a separate piece of paper, draw a compass for the client and identify each direction. Explain that North does not change with the learner's location, but is a set direction that is important to know because it helps you understand where other places are in relation to it. Help the learner memorize the directional compass by offering a rhyme, like "Never Eat Soggy Waffles," for North, East, South, and West.

3) Begin with where the client is currently staying or working. Ask the learner if he can find this place on the map. Help him find it.

4) From there, ask him where he would like to go or to name a place he goes often. Ask him to identify where this place is on the map. Now that the two places are identified, ask which direction he would be traveling toward if he left from point A and headed to point B.

5) With the learner, brainstorm a series of hypothetical situations in which he would start from one location and travel to another. Ask which direction he would be heading towards and which train or bus he would take to get there.

6) Review everything that was covered with the maps on Google Maps, using the Directions button. This is another tool for the learner to check himself and to easily locate directions if he has to get someplace in a hurry.

This activity never gets old and is always good to review with the learner, especially if he is about to venture somewhere that is unfamiliar. Often learners are too embarrassed to admit that they don't really understand directions or how to get where they need to go. Because of this fear, they often stay close to home and are reluctant to visit new places. Overcoming this hurdle is essential if the learner is trying to make a significant change in his life.

Your Vote Is Your Voice

Is the learner registered to vote? What are the voting laws in your state? In New York, people with felony convictions have the right to vote just like anyone else, but those who are still on parole are forced to wait. Many of my clients were surprised to learn they still had the right to vote. Find out what your state's laws are and discuss them with the learner. Discuss why exercising the right to vote is important. What are the issues the learner cares most about? How do politics directly impact her life?

Download a voting application and help the learner complete it and mail it in. After the learner becomes registered, make sure she understands where her local poll site is located.

NUMERACY LESSONS

Creating a Budget

The aim of this activity is to alleviate stress by writing down the learner's financial needs and guidelines for each month, week, and day. It seems like a common sense tool, but many people do not track their spending and feel so discouraged about their financial situation that they avoid dealing with it by spending what little income they receive on frivolous items, like lottery tickets.

Creating a budget is an essential tool for everyone, especially for those who are trying to overcome poverty.

Part 1: Make a list of expenses

1) Have the learner recall expenses from today, yesterday, and each day of this week. Make a list of every expense. Example:

2) Today: $1.00 soda, $5.00 Metrocard, $1.50 coffee.
3) Add the expenses for each day and for the week.
4) Multiply this list by four. This shows a snapshot of an approximate amount of money the learner is spending per month.
5) Discuss which, if any, expenses surprised the learner. For instance, when I did this exercise with a class I learned that I was spending about $8.00 a week on cans of soda. This exercise helped me realize how much I was spending on this unhealthy and frivolous item and it helped me cut down on calories and saved money.
6) Discuss the difference between necessities and luxuries.
7) Encourage the learner to carry an envelope or folder and collect receipts for a week or two to get in better practice of keeping track of expenses.

Part 2: List Necessities
1) Make a list of expenses that are absolutely crucial, such as rent, utilities, cell phone bill, transportation costs, childcare costs, prescriptions, and groceries. Add the approximate amount each expense adds up to in one month.
2) Discuss how that figure is the bare minimum that the learner will have to make or if she's already employed, she will have to make sure she saves enough of her income to cover those key expenses.
3) What is the learner's current income? How much does she receive in each paycheck? Does she receive any public assistance or food stamps, and if so, how much? How much more will she have to make in order to meet her bottom line expenses?
4) Subtract the total amount for expenses from the learner's paycheck income or total income. How much is left over? Part of this amount could be put aside for savings. Have the learner brainstorm situations or items that savings are sometimes used towards.

5) Divide the amount that is left over by four. This is the extra amount the learner has to work with each week. Then divide this amount by 5 or 7 to determine how much the learner can spend each day.
6) Discuss how the budget can help the learner save and plan for the future. Try to remind the learner that while the numbers may present a bleak picture at the moment, knowing what they are and developing a plan for the future is the first step towards changing them for the better.

Credit Check

Many of us dread thinking about our credit histories, but the first step in improving your credit score is confronting what's lurking in your credit background. Fortunately, these scores can be improved upon. If the learner is interested in renting or buying a home or a car, he will want to make sure he knows what's in his report because his credit will be checked by prospective loan agents. Even some employers check credit these days, which is outrageous and will hopefully be outlawed someday.

Even if the learner has no interest in buying anything, the Federal Trade Commission recommends checking your credit once a year to make sure your identity hasn't been stolen.

Each year everyone is allowed one free credit report from each of the three credit reporting agencies: Experian, TransUnion, and Equifax. There are a lot of scammers out there who claim to offer free credit reports, but either charge a fee or steal consumers' identities or both. The only authorized website is www.AnnualCreditReport.com. Never click on pop-up ads that offer free credit checks.

Help the learner complete the online or mail-in credit form and review the results with the learner.

If you find that there are discrepancies or the learner's identity has been stolen, visit the Federal Trade Commission's website for instruction on how to dispute the report's claim: www.ftc.gov.

If there are legitimate issues of past debt, you can help the learner write a letter to the business in question, explaining that he intends to pay it back and is interested in working out a payment plan. Sometimes this helps to stall the interest accumulation.

My former clients and I have been very fortunate to work with financial coaching leaders from the Community Service Society in New York: Reyes Irizarry, Jerry Silverman, and Jeremy Koch, who are much more knowledgeable about this process and other financial literacy issues.

Real Life Math Worksheet 1
Sam's Spectacular Workweek

1) You have a cold and still have to work, so you're going to take medicine. You can take two caplets every six hours. What is the maximum number of pills you can take in one day?

2) You are making Thanksgiving dinner for your entire family. The normal recipe, which serves 4 people, calls for ¾ cups of chopped onions, and 3 cups of stuffing, ½ cup of flour. How many cups of chopped onions, stuffing, and flour will you need to make enough stuffing for 12 people?

Congratulations! You just got a new job and will be working this shift:

Mon	Tue	Wed	Thu	Fri	Sat	Sun
8:30 4:30	7:00 3:00	10:00 6:00	8:00 4:00	Off	9:00 5:00	Off

3) How many hours will you work each week?

4) If you receive $10.50 an hour, what will you make before taxes in one week?

5) How much will you make in one month before taxes?

6) Overtime is usually time and a half, meaning your hourly plus half of your hourly. If you work an average of 3 hours of overtime each week, how much more will you make (before taxes)?

It's a new job and you're trying to get to know the neighborhood and your coworkers. This is the amount of money you've spent on lunch in your first week:

Mon	Tue	Wed	Thu	Fri	Sat	Sun
$5.50	$11.00	$6.50	$7.00	$0	$8.50	$0

7) How much did you spend this week on lunch?

8) What is the average amount of money you spent on lunch during your workweek?

9) Do you think it would be more economical to pack your lunch? List three ideas for a packed lunch that would cost less than going out to eat?

10) You take the subway to and from work every day, plus you use the subway to attend meetings twice a week. Which is the most economical Metrocard to purchase?

Your monthly expenses are:

Rent	$500
Metrocard	$104
Phone bill	$83.27
Con Edison	$68.73
Laundry	$30.00

11) How much in total will you spend on expenses?

12) How much will you have left over for groceries and other expenses?

Real Life Math Worksheet 1
Sam's Spectacular Workweek
Answers

1) 8
2) 2 ¼ cups of chopped onions, 9 cups of stuffing, 1½ cups of flour.
3) 40 hours
4) $420
5) $1,680
6) $47.25
7) $38.50
8) $7.70
9) Yes, and something like: a sandwich, leftovers from home, or a salad from home.
10) This question should be tailored to your local transportation. In New York, the unlimited monthly plan is the most economical, but many of us do not have $104 at one time so we have to spend $29 per week for an unlimited card until we have that $104 saved.
11) $786
12) $894 (before taxes)

Real Life Math Worksheet 2
Peter's Super-Rad Pizzeria

Congratulations! You've been hired at Peter's Super-Rad Pizzeria!

You make $7.50 an hour and are a full-time employee. Occasionally, you will have to put in extra time based on deadlines and baking schedules. When you work overtime you need to keep track of your hours so the company knows to pay you.

This week your time card looked like this:

Mon	Tue	Wed	Thu	Fri	Sat	Sun
6:00	5:30	6:00	6:00	8:00	Off	5:30
3:00	2:00	3:00	2:00	4:00		6:30

1) What do you make when you work 40 hours a week (before taxes)?

2) How many hours did you work in total this week?

3) How many hours of overtime did you work?

4) If the overtime rate is the same as your hourly rate, how much more money did you make (compared to the normal 40-hour work week)?

5) If the overtime rate is the same as your hourly rate, how much in total does the company owe you this week (before taxes)?

6) Without counting any possible overtime this month, what would be your normal take-home income (before taxes)?

7) Let's say you're looking to move into a new apartment. Before you begin to search for a new home you will need to figure out approximately, how much of your monthly income should go towards rent. How much, ideally, would you like to budget for rent?

8) How much money do you have left over for other expenses after rent?

Real Life Math Worksheet 2
<u>Peter's Super-Rad Pizzeria</u>
Answers

1) $300
2) 55 ½ hours
3) Answer: 15 ½ hours
4) Answer: $116.25
5) Answer: $416.25
6) Answer: $1,200
7) Answer: This will vary, depending on where you live. Generally, it's ideal to keep the amount of rent to within half of your monthly income: $600.
8) Answer: $600

Real Life Math Worksheet 3
Tom's Take What's Yours: Time and Money Management Activity

1) You have a new job and you're about to cash your first paycheck. Your paycheck is for the amount $450. The cash-checking place takes 5% of your check. How much will that be?

2) After the check-cashing place cashes your check, how much of your check will you actually receive?

3) You decide to go to a different check-cashing place. Instead of charging a percent of the check, they charge a flat rate: $4 for every hundred dollars. How much will they charge you?

4) Explanation of the previous question: How many hundreds are there?

5) If you use the second cash-checking place, how much of your check will you actually receive?

6) Which cash-checking place will give you back more of your check?

7) If you return to the same cash-checking place, how much of your money will you give them in one month's time?

8) If you keep using them to cash your checks, how much money will you give them in one year?

9) How much does your current cash-checking place charge?

10) How much of your check do you give them each time you cash a check?

11) How much will you give that cash-checking place in one month?

12) How much will you give them in 6 months? A year?

13) Is there a way to cash your check without having to give any of it to the company that cashes it for you?

14) What do we mean by fee-free? Is it true that banks charge money, even though it's my hard-earned money and even though they've done a credit check?

15) What does ATM stand for?

16) Sometimes banks charge $5.00 a month if you make three or more withdrawals. So it's better to withdrawal a bigger amount at one time rather than each time you need funds.

17) ATMs that belong to other banks will charge you a fee to use their machine. Often there is a fee that your bank charges too. Most ATMs of other banks charge $2.50 and then your bank will charge anywhere from $2.00 to $2.50 per withdrawal. How much in total is taken from your account if you use an ATM from another bank?

Real Life Math Worksheet 3
Tom's Take What's Yours: Time and Money Management Activity
Answers

1) $22.50
2) $427.50
3) $20
4) There are five because $27.50 counts as the next hundred. Multiply five times $4.
5) $407.50
6) The second one.
7) $80
8) $960
9) Depends on client's information.
10) Depends on client's information
11) Depends on client's information
12) Depends on client's information
13) Yes, at a bank or credit union. Discuss monthly fees and help find out if a bank or credit union offers a fee-free account.
14) Fee-free means there is no fee to open your bank account. Some banks also require a minimum amount, like $250 to start with before they will open an account.
15) Automatic Telling Machine. Discuss the functions they serve.
16) This wasn't really a question.
17) $4.50 to $5.00

Real Life Math Worksheet 4
Carolyn's Making Change &
Counting Money Activity

For the following, please determine the amount of change to give back with fewest bills and coins:

1) If your total is $106.73 and the customer gives you 1 hundred dollar bill and 1 ten, how much will you give back?

2) If the total is $127.34 and you the customer hands you 7 twenties, what will you hand back?

3) If the total is $43.75, and the customer gives you 2 twenties and a ten, how much change do you give back?

4) If the total is $27.94 and the customer gives you 2 twenties, how much change do you give back?

5) If the total is $43.78 and the customer gives you 3 twenties?

6) If the total is $31.94 and the customer gives you 2 twenties?

7) If the total is $70.25 and the customer hands you 4 twenties?

8) If the total is $1.29 and the customer hands you 1 five?

9) If the total is $79.83 and the customer hands you 1 fifty, 1 twenty, and 1 ten?

10) If the total is $35.00 and the customer gives you 1 hundred?

11) If the total is $42.67 and the customer gives you 2 twenties and 1 ten?

12) If the total is $53.82 and the customer gives you 3 twenties?

13) If the total is $106.45 and the customer gives you 2 fifties and 1 twenty?

14) If the total is $10.12 and the customer gives you 1 twenty?

15) If the total is $36.00 and the customer gives you 2 twenties?

16) If the total is $54.96 and the customer gives you 3 twenties?

17) If the total is $78.29 and the customer gives you 4 twenties?

18) If the total is $19.50 and the customer gives you 1 twenty?

19) If the total is $68.21 and the customer gives you 4 twenties?

20) If the total is $123.72 and the customer gives you 3 fifties?

21) If the total is $57.03 and the customer gives you 3 twenties?

22) If the total is $75.78 and the customer gives you 4 twenties?

23) If the total is $39.76 and the customer gives you 2 twenties?

24) If the total is $83.29 and the customer gives you 1 hundred bill?

25) If the total is $ 67.23 and the customer gives you 4 twenties?

26) If the total is $109.67 and the customer gives you 6 twenties?

27) If the total is $43.63 and the customer gives you 3 twenties?

28) If the total is $2.16 and the customer gives you 1 five?

29) If the total is $3.62 and the customer gives you 1 five?

30) If the total is $17.46 and the customer gives you 1 twenty?

Real Life Math Worksheet 4
<u>Carolyn's Making Change &</u>
<u>Counting Money Activity</u>
Answers

1) $3.27 = 3 ones, 1 quarter, 2 pennies.
2) $12.16 = 1 ten, two ones, a dime a nickel and 1 penny.
3) $6.25 = 1 five, 1 one, and a quarter.
4) $12.06 = 1 ten, 2 ones, a nickel and a penny.
5) $16.22 = 1 ten, 1 five, 1 one, 2 dimes and 2 pennies.
6) $8.06 = 1 five, 3 ones, 1 nickel, and 1 penny.
7) $9.75 = 1 five, 4 ones, 3 quarters.
8) $3.71 = 3 ones, 2 quarters, 2 dimes and 1 penny.
9) $.17 = 1 dime, 1 nickel and 2 pennies.
10) $65 = 3 twenties and 1 five.
11) $7.33 = 1 five, 2 ones, 1 quarter, 1 nickel, 3 pennies.
12) $6.18 = 1 five, 1 one, 1 dime, 1 nickel, and three pennies.
13) $13.55 = 1 ten, 3 ones, 2 quarters, and 1 nickel.
14) $9.88 = 1 five, 4 ones, 3 quarters, 1 dime, and 3 pennies.
15) $4.00 = 4 ones.
16) $5.04 = 1 five, 4 pennies.
17) $1.71 = 1 one, 2 quarters, 2 dimes and 1 penny.
18) $.50 = 2 quarters.
19) $11.79 = 1 ten, 1 one, 3 quarters, 4 pennies.
20) $21.28 = 1 twenty, 1 one, 1 quarter, 3 pennies.
21) $2.97= 2 ones, 3 quarters, 2 dimes, 2 pennies.
22) $1.22 = 1 one, 2 dimes, 2 pennies.
23) $.24 = 2 dimes, 4 pennies.
24) $16.71 = 1 ten, 1 five, 1 one, 2 quarters, 2 dimes, and 1 penny.
25) $12.77 = 1 ten, 2 ones, 3 quarters, 2 pennies.
26) $10.33 = 1 ten, 1 quarter, 1 nickel, 3 pennies.
27) $16.37 = 1 ten, 1 five, 1 one, 1 quarter, 1 dime, 2 pennies.
28) $2.84 = 2 ones, 3 quarters, 1 nickel, 4 pennies.
29) $1.38 = 1 one, 1 quarter, 1 dime, 3 pennies.
30) $2.54 = 2 ones, 2 quarters, and 4 pennies.

Real Life Math Worksheet 5
Gabriel's Groovy Candy Store

You are the new cashier at Gabriel's Groovy Candy Store! Everything is going really well, except the cash register's calculator is broken.

Here are the prices for the following items:

Jelly beans	$7.99 lb
Gummy worms	$2.99 lb
Peanut Butter Cups	$1.99
Bubble Gum	$0.50
Rainbow Jumbo Lollipop	$4.50
Teddy Bear	$35.00
Balloon	$5.00

You will encounter a number of demanding customers. Take your time and add up each order. Take turns playing the cashier or customer and make up a number of orders.

Here are the three steps for each scenario:

1) Add up the total.

2) Deduct the 8.875% sales tax (or the percentage of your local tax).

3) Determine which bills the customer pays with and then identify the least number of bills and coins you will give back to the customer.

Real Life Math Worksheet 6
<u>Stephen's Paycheck Lesson</u>

Gross pay is what you make before any **deductions**. If a job is advertised at $30,000 a year, then that's the **gross pay**.

Net pay is what's left AFTER taxes, health benefits and other deductions are taken out of your check. So gross pay of $30,000 would become something like net pay of $22,564.

FICA is **Federal Insurance Contributions Act (FICA) tax**. This funds social security and Medicare and disability insurance, like SSI.

Ask the learner to use a recent paycheck to calculate the following:

1) In a year, how much will you pay in FICA?

2) In a year, how much will you pay in State Withholding Tax?

3) In a year, how much will you pay in Health Insurance?

4) In a year, how much will you pay in Federal Withholding Tax?

Computer Literacy

We are living in the digital age. Most jobs now require a basic understanding of how to use a computer and the Internet. Even the state's Human Resources Administration, the bureau that distributes food stamps and supplemental income to those who are living in poverty requires the recipients to conduct online job searches each week. This can be daunting to those who did not have access to computers and many often feel as though the world has passed them by and they can never catch up.

Our job is to show each learner how the Internet can actually make his life easier.

First, ask the learner about his interests. If he can't think of any, ask him if he likes to follow the news. Almost everyone says, "yes" to this question. Ask him for his favorite newspaper or channel and then find it for him on the computer. Let him take in the information and explain how he can "click" on "links," and find out even more information.

Explain that each page on the Internet has its own address just like the building surrounding us. Then introduce the address bar. Encourage the learner to look up anything in the world, get him to experiment with the cursor, mouse or mouse pad, before moving on to a list of real life goals.

The Computer Literacy Checklist is more job-search focused, but it should be modified to meet each learner's specific goals.

Computer Literacy Checklist

_____ Locate and read the daily news
_____ Create an email address
_____ Connect with friends and family with social media
_____ Navigate a trip using driving directions or public transportation by using Google Maps or another website
_____ Demonstrate proficiency with online job search engines
_____ Compose a job inquiry cover letter in email form
_____ Know how to download and upload your resume
_____ Email resume and cover letter to at least 5 prospective employers

1. _____

2. _____

3. _____

4. _____

5. _____

_____ Fill out at least one online job application
_____ Pass the Computer Literacy Test comprised of computer literacy terms

Computer Literacy Test

1) Which is an example of an Internet or web browser?
   A. Firefox
   B. Chrome
   C. Internet Explorer
   D. All of the above

2) Which is a definition of an address bar / navigation bar?
   A. A feature in a web browser that is at the top of the page and lists the exact location or URL of the web page.
   B. It means a bar that has many addresses.
   C. It's where I type my password to get into my email account.
   D. None of the above

3) Which is an example of an email address?
   A. http://www.LiteracyIsPower.com
   B. MurphysLaw11
   C. PlummerForHire@gmail.com
   D. None of the above

4) I must _____ my resume to an online job application form.
   A. delete
   B. upload
   C. download
   D. None of the above

5) If I want to log into my email what is the first step?
   A. Check Craigslist for new job ads.
   B. Type the website address that hosts my email account in the address bar.
   C. Restart the computer.
   D. All of the above

6) If my email address is JanetJobSeeker@gmail.com and my password is HairMetalBands4ever!, what do I type into the Username field on the Gmail website?

   A. @
   B. HairMetalBands4ever
   C. JanetJobSeeker
   D. None of the above.

7) What must I always remember to do after I've been checking my email on a public computer?

   A. Restart the computer.
   B. Sign out.
   C. Visit a different website.
   D. Stick my gum under the desk.

8) If I want to send a brand new email, what button to I click when I'm signed into my Gmail account?

   A. Inbox
   B. Reply
   C. Compose
   D. Sent

9) Name the part of the computer that controls my cursor.

   A. URL
   B. Mouse
   C. Computer Screen
   D. USB thumb drive

10) If I decide not to attach the cover letter to my email, I should paste it into the _____.

   A. Atmosphere
   B. Abyss
   C. Body of the email
   D. The dictionary

11) How do I copy and paste?
    A. Highlight the item I want copied and pasted.
    B. Move the cursor to where I would like it to be pasted.
    C. Click command or "apple" C to copy and then command or "apple" V to paste.
    D. All of the above

12) If I want to do a general search on the Internet to look something up, what is the best website to visit?
    A. Facebook
    B. Twitter
    C. Google
    D. MySpace

13) What is an example of a website to conduct an online job search?
    A. www.craigslist.org
    B. www.monster.com
    C. www.idealist.org
    D. All of the above

14) In my email cover letter, which I'm writing in the body of the email, how do I address the prospective employer whose name is Michael Smith?
    A. To Whom It May Concern:
    B. Dear Mr. Smith,
    C. Dear Mr. Michael Smith,
    D. All of the above

TRUE or FALSE

15) Just because something is posted on the Internet doesn't mean it's a legitimate job ad.
   A. True
   B. False

16) If you receive an email congratulating you on being hired and you have never met with the person it's from, though you did send your resume to them, then it's most likely a scam.
   A. True
   B. False

17) If it's from a company I've heard of then it's okay to give my bank information to the representative on the phone or on email.
   A. True
   B. False

18) If the job ad states that no experience is necessary and offers to pay $30 an hour it is probably a scam.
   A. True
   B. False

19) If I send my resume and cover letter to an ad and it turns out to be a hoax, then my identity will definitely be stolen.
   A. True
   B. False

20) Most legitimate job leads will require me to pay a fee for placement or administrative costs.
   A. True
   B. False

Fill In The Blank

The next two questions refer to the ad pasted below.

21) List the date it was posted: _____

22) If I wanted to apply for this job, how would I contact the person? _____

GroundsKeepers (Brooklyn)

Date: 2013-11-15, 10:39AM EST
Reply to: job186@JoesList.com

Groundskeepers Needed For New Apartment Complex
*Full Time Position at $10 per hour
*Full Benefits-Health, Dental, Vacation, and Holiday Pay
*Monday thru Friday Work Schedule

o   Location: Brooklyn
o   Compensation: $10/hr
o   Principals only. Recruiters, please don't contact this job poster.
o   Please, no phone calls about this job!
o   Please do not contact job poster about other services, products or commercial interests.

SPOT THE SCAM

23) The following ad is a scam. Examine the ad below and give at least three examples of how we know this is not a legitimate job ad.

    1. _____

    2. _____

    3. _____

LOOKING FOR SECURITY GUARDS FOR CORPORATE &
RETAILS...IMMIDIATE HIRE.. (MR.ORTIZ- 917-427-2431)

Date: 2013-11-17, 10:57 AM EST
Reply to: job2349@JoesList.com

SAME DAY INTERVIEW……

CALL TODAY TO SCHEDULE YOUR INTERVIEW FOR THIS WEEK

looking for reliable security guards to work in a corporate environment
we will put you to work as long as you have the proper training
if you have no training we will train you
i only deal with corporate sites : hospitals, hotels, airports, office buildings and many more
you must be available to work a.s.a.p
we have full time and part time positions available

if your interested please contact MR.ORTIZ at 917-427-2431

we are one of the best companies and we have job sites in all 5-boroughs of NYC
you must be 18 years and older, and most important you must have a clean background (no felonies, no parole, no probation)
if your already trained all you need is a job …. CALL TODAY

contact Mr.Ortiz AT 917-427-2431

thank you in advance for considering our company
if your interested please call us so that we could
schedule an interview with you ...remember, first
impression is the main one so hope to see you soon.
there is a probation period for 3 months....after your 3
months probation you'll get health and dental benefits,
pay vacations and pay holidays and possible a pay
raise
email replies should contain full name and contact info
please

looking for security 24/hrs
must be 18 and older
must have a clean background
must be able to work a.s.a.p
we have sites in all 5 boroughs,
new york, new jersey, long island
we have part-time and full-time
morning, afternoon, and evening shifts
the starting pay is $10-up to $18 an hour
for more info contact HR DEPARTMENT: 917-427-2431
you will be on a 3 month probation period,
after your 3 month probation period you will get
health, dental benefits pay vacations and pay holidays
must be filled a.s.a.p
call today to schedule an appointment

CALL MR.Ortiz AT 917-427-2431

Computer Literacy Test
Answer Key

1) D
2) A
3) C
4) B
5) B
6) C
7) B
8) C
9) B
10) C
11) D
12) C
13) D
14) D, but C is the best one to use.
15) A
16) A
17) B
18) A
19) B
20) B
21) November 15, 2013
22) Send an email to the email listed at the top
23) Acceptable answers include: Spelling typos in title, grammatical problems throughout, the fact that only a cell phone number is listed, "if you have no training we will train you." And "remember, first impression is the main one so hope to see you soon." The ad is working too hard to lure us in. If it were legit, it would simply state facts.

Chapter 12
Fundraising

"Anyone who has ever struggled with poverty knows how extremely expensive it is to be poor." –James Baldwin

A widely discussed and debated issue within the literacy education community is whether learners should be charged for instruction. It is my (very strong) opinion that literacy instruction should be free of charge because many learners are already living in poverty and even if they aren't living in poverty, a fee could serve as a deterrent and discourage learners from pursuing their goals.

If you are operating as an individual instructor, it should not cost much beyond carfare and an hour of your time each week to provide one-on-one literacy instruction and this chapter will be of little use to you. However, if you are trying to start your own literacy program within an established organization, it would benefit you to help your organization apply for literacy grants to cover the cost of books, supplies, and perhaps even some paid instructors and coordinators. Funding can help your organization grow and reach even more learners.

Keep in mind that your funding strategy greatly influences how you measure literacy progress (see Chapter 8). First, your organization needs to determine whether it will apply for government funding or not because this decision will tell you whether you will use standardized tests or be able to use a materials or performance-based measure. If your organization decides to pursue government funding then you can start by reading about their specific standards and follow their guidelines.

Government funding doesn't just mean the Department of Education. Be creative. Demonstrate the connection between literacy and other issues like the environment or energy. Dr. Stephen Reder of Portland State University offered a brilliant idea for funding during his lecture on digital literacy at ProLiteracy's US Conference on Adult Literacy. He explained that the FCC has been charging telephone consumers a Universal Access charge for years, from back when we needed to get telephones out to rural communities. That need has already been fulfilled, but they are still collecting those "Universal Access" fees. Now "Universal Access" can include broadband. This means we can ask for federal money from the US Department of Urban Housing, Corporation for National Service, Department of Energy, and the other federal agencies that approved the bill. We can use this money to support digital literacy. If your organization serves learners who are trying to gain employment, you could also reach out to the Department of Labor or your local government's employment department.

Fundraising is about creating partnerships. Whether you are asking for a book donation or a six-figure grant to grow your program, you are offering an opportunity to the donor to participate in creating a lasting positive change. Create regional consortiums comprised of business and government groups who would be interested in contributing to adult or teen literacy.

An example of partnership fundraising is posting on your organization's website how a donation will go towards paper, pencils, books, or create an online literacy registry so partners can see exactly where their contribution is going.

Consider your organization's mission. What populations do you serve? How many do you serve? What is the range of ages? Many foundations or private donors are quite particular about supporting programs that are solely for youth while others support programs devoted to adult and others support family literacy. Identify your organization's perimeters so you will be able to implement a literacy program that builds upon the mission and connects the mission with the interests of potential funders.

While every foundation has different requirements I recommend doing some grant research while you plan your program so you can implement a literacy program that will produce results that most donors would consider supporting.

Whether you are seeking government or private funding you will need to implement a literacy program that is structured in a way that can be measured (see Chapter 8). In the very beginning you will only be able to offer the numbers of learners served and the number of instructional hours, but over time as you get a system in place, you will be able to collect more data that paints a more detailed picture of your program's literacy progress.

There are a number of local and national foundations that support literacy. It's usually easier to apply for smaller grants from smaller foundations or from individual donors. You can find these people and foundations by searching for "literacy" and/or "education" and your town's name. Also, visit the Foundation Center's website and do the same search there. Research where other local nonprofits are finding support. I recommend visiting *The Chronicle of Philanthropy*'s website for insightful articles and weekly grant leads.

Here is a list of larger foundations and organizations that support literacy:

- American Library Association
- Literacy Funders Network
- Foundation for Family Literacy
- Dollar General Literacy Foundation
- Donors Choose
- Barnes & Noble Booksellers, Sponsorships and Charitable Donations
- National Endowment for the Humanities
- International Reading Association
- The NEA Foundation
- National Education Foundation
- Verizon Foundation
- Target Stores
- Starbucks Youth Action Grants
- The Barbara Bush Foundation for Family Literacy
- Wallace Foundation
- The John D. and Catherine T. MacArthur Foundation
- John S. and James L. Knight Foundation
- Open Society's Campaign for Black Male Achievement
- Carnegie Corporation of New York
- Bill & Melinda Gates Foundation
- The Pew Charitable Trusts
- Ford Foundation – financial literacy
- The William and Flora Hewlett Foundation

Each foundation asks specific questions and operates within its own criteria. Your pitch, whether this is a verbal or written request for money, should do two things, it: 1.) presents the story or problem and 2.) offers a solution that involves the donor's contribution.

There are a number of resources available on the Internet about how to write a grant. The specifics will come from the foundation itself. However, most grant proposals will include these elements:

o   Research – the proposal will demonstrate both quantitative and qualitative research that presents the problem of illiteracy in your geographic region.
o   Methodology & Mission – the proposal will describe the goals for the specific project that the donor will be funding and exactly how your organization plans to track and measure this progress.
o   Timeline – how long will it take for the project to complete its mission?
o   Information outreach – how will your program disseminate the information gained by this project and contribute to the larger picture of fighting against illiteracy?
o   Materials & Budget – what exactly will your organization require in order to meet the proposed project's goals and how much will it cost, item by item and in total?

Don't forget to follow up with a thank you note, especially when you are awarded funds.

Chapter 13
The Future

*"Education is our passport to the future, for tomorrow belongs to the people who prepare for it today." –**Malcom X***

The United Nations Education, Science and Cultural Organization (UNESCO) declared that literacy is a human right and in 2003 they established the United Nations Literacy Decade. One of UNESCO's literacy goals is to reach a 50% improvement rate for adult literacy by 2015 and for all children to have access to education. Obviously, the fight against illiteracy and poverty will take much longer, but by making literacy an urgent priority we can mobilize the world to start taking action.

Over 90 million Americans have basic or below basic literacy skills. This costs the US hundreds of billions of dollars each year. More than half of the US prison population has below basic or basic literacy skills, according to the American Institutes for Reasearch report, "Preparing for Life Beyond Prison Walls: The Literacy of Incarcerated Adults Near Release." How are these individuals supposed to rejoin community and pursue legitimate work if they cannot read or write? Without any action, the economy, education system, criminal justice system, and healthcare problems will continue to get worse.

Illiteracy is a widespread crisis that hits upon every major social and economic issue. Literacy triage is in order and it can easily be conducted by anyone who cares enough to do something about the problem.

What you can do:

1) Teach. Tutor someone who needs to build literacy skills. Follow the Seven Steps for a Successful Session and directly participate in change.
2) Promote learner ambassadors. Encourage others to give back and teach others how to build their literacy skills. The most effective teachers and advocates of the power of literacy are teen or adult learners who have overcome the barriers of illiteracy themselves. When learner ambassadors share their stories with policy makers or prospective literacy supporters, the issue becomes real for the audience and reaches them on a more personal level.
3) Raise awareness. Document what you have learned as a literacy activist and share your findings with others. Promote literacy by letting others know what worked and didn't work for you and your organization.
4) Partner with other organizations. The problem of illiteracy is widespread and should not be framed as an issue that polarizes people into presubscribed categories. It is faster and easier to work together. Rather than rebuild something that is working, support other organizations that are already making strides by adding your knowledge, experience, and support.
5) Advocate. Pay attention to education and economic policies and do what you can to influence change, whether that's voting, voicing your opinion, investing in projects that make a difference, or sharing your success stories with others.

For me, being a literacy activist is by far the most enriching work I've ever had the privilege of doing. The courage and strength I have seen learners exhibit is beyond inspiring. Working with learners, teens and adults, has taught me what is possible when a person makes a decision to change, to improve themselves and the world. Our decisions in this life really do matter and we can overcome unfortunate circumstances.

Some of the success stories I have had the honor to witness and help facilitate involve learners going from homelessness to securing employment and housing, starting as a ward of the state to regaining independence and reuniting with their children, unable to recite the alphabet to reading bedtime stories to their grandchildren. One of the learners I worked with began on a pre-alphabet level and now writes poetry and regularly does public speaking, inspiring those who are in recovery from chemical dependency. Another learner was unable to write his address when we started working together and now he works as a courier, delivering important packages all over New York City.

I continue to learn from those I work with and organizations dedicated to fighting illiteracy and poverty. Here are some great informational resources on literacy:

o UNESCO
o American Library Association
o Literacy Information and Communication System (LINCS)
o International Reading Association
o National Center for Educational Statistics
o National Assessment of Adult Literacy
o National Coalition for Literacy
o National Center for Family Literacy
o National Education Association
o ProLiteracy

Education is an investment in the future. It's a long-term investment that makes an immediate and serious short-term impact on everyday life. Everyone has something to offer to the literacy movement and the time to act is now.

Visit us and share your stories:

o   www.LiteracyIsPower.com
o   www.facebook.com/LiteracyIsPower
o   @LiteracyPower

Acknowledgements

This book was written for all the learners out there. I have learned from those I have worked with and I'm inspired each day by your courage and perseverance. Out of respect for your privacy, I will not mention you by name. You know who you are.

My husband, Peter W. Slattery, gave me the idea for this book and without his help, love, and encouragement it would never have been written. He also created and designed the cover art, proofread and formatted the book, and I thank him with all of my heart.

Special thanks also to M.C. Lewis, author of *Spin Doctor*, which was a Quarterfinalist in Amazon's Breakthrough Novel Award Competition and a must-read. M.C. Lewis has influenced me on countless levels, even proofread the book, and offered invaluable insight and encouragement from the start to finish of this process.

I want to thank the great literary hero, Jimmy Santiago Baca, author of *A Glass of Water* and *A Place To Stand*, and many other renowned works, whose writing is a lifeline for so many. He inspires the world to take their lives into their own hands and create change through words. I am eternally grateful for his work and for his support.

Thank you to Pablo Eisenberg for his indispensable work that is reshaping the nonprofit and philanthropic worlds. I am truly honored to have his support.

I am also grateful to Nikhil Goyal, author of *One Size Does Not Fit All: A Student's Assessment of School*. His work is a motivating and important influence to the future and I thank him for his support.

I owe a special thanks to my parents, Charles Lewis and Pamela Gilbert, for being modern-day heroes who fight each day for truth and justice. I thank them for their endless support and for teaching me to always follow my dreams.

Thanks to my brother, Gabriel G. Lewis, for being so brilliant and cool, for always providing great music, humor, and new ideas. To me, he is an example of why it is important to listen to members of the younger generations. They're more than just the future.

Thank you also to our family: Dorothy Lewis, Elaine Gilbert, Murray Gilbert, Randy Fisher, Mary Lewis, Dorothy Fisher, Tom Fisher, Evan Roe, Robin Gilbert, Jim McAuliffe, Peter McAuliffe, Cathy and Philip Bunting, Jim, Cheryle, and Matthew Bunting, Brandon and Nicole Bunting, Eugene and Margaret Kelechava, Ruth Miller, Franklin Cherry, Elizabeth Durham, Joe Burton, Jay Worrall, Chel Avery, Daniel Worrall, Paige Scoltock Worrall, Michael Worrall, Clara Lesher Worrall, Kelly Worrall, Jay Worrall, Michelle Worrall, DJ McGuire, John McGuire, Megan Reilly, Aileen Wessel, and the Worrall children: Stephen, Sam, Carolyn, Jay, Clayton, Wesley, and Gabriel.

I am indebted to Barbara Darne and Ed Wahler for all of their great work with Bastille Arts and for their support.

I had the honor of working with Robyn Olds, an extraordinarily talented art therapist and literacy instructor and she inspired many of the ideas that are in this book and helped put them into practice.

Other literacy leaders and educators that I owe an extra special thanks to are: Samantha Smith, Anji Janitschek, Michele Schuster, Ana Vasquez, Vanessa Lozano, Tamara Spears, David "Bucco" Senecal, Manny Fernandez, Dr. Brian Dybowski, Dr. Richard Bank, Steve Hannum, David Whitaker, Todd Evans, Mary McGonegal, David Harvey, Dr. Stephen Reder, Kelly Thieme, Karen Ray, Nell Eckersley, Adam Kaplan, Ben James, Annie Crowder, Reyes Irrizarry, Jerry Silverman, Jeremy Koch, and Howard Pflanzer.

Finally, I would like to thank these friends and colleagues for their inspiring work: Sheila Kaplan, Mary Balaban, Tamara Bates, Rhea DeRose Weiss, Faiza Bukhari, Robert Herring, John Ellert, Harvey Semler, Steve Martin, Robert Bowman, Vance Lawson, Ben Kalish, Mike Ross, Jessica Cannold, Maureen Cavanaugh, Christine Stavem, Lisa Gray, Taylor Green, Jen Liang, Adrian Paul, Angie Doss, and to all those who are out there trying to make a difference.

www.ingramcontent.com/pod-product-compliance
Lightning Source LLC
LaVergne TN
LVHW021342080426
835508LV00020B/2071